Unrequited

Matt-
This is the first Copy of
Unrequited that I've signed.
It's message is very near + dear
to my heart.

Enjoy,

A. K

Unrequited

Things I Learned from Trying to Love The Wrong People

Andrew Kendall

ISBN: 0692047514
ISBN 13: 9780692047514

**Also by
Andrew Kendall:**

The Dark Dictionary: A Guide to Help Eradicate Your
Darkness, Restore Your Light, and Redefine Your Life

To my heart—for everything I, as well as others, put you through.

And to those I gave a little piece of my heart to—thanks for the content, but here's where I take my power back.

"How many people do you have to fall in love with until you finally understand that the only person you owe yourself to… is you?"

R.M. DRAKE

"I love you, in a really, really big–pretend
to like your taste in music, let you eat the
last piece of cheesecake, hold a radio over
my head outside your window–unfortunate
way that makes me hate you, love you.
So pick me. Choose me. Love me."

GREY'S ANATOMY, 2005.

"Don't let what he wants eclipse what
you need. He is very dreamy, but
he is not the sun... you are."

GREY'S ANATOMY, 2014.

It's time to leave it all behind
It's time to pick up the pieces of my scattered mind
And after all my petals fall
I can finally find beauty beneath once and for all

I've spent way too long judging myself
Running from truth into someone else's arms
But I'm done, the battle's begun, the battle's begun

There's fire in me, deep down in my veins
These clouds in my head, they're not gonna rain
There's fight in my heart, there's hope in my eyes
There's hope in my eyes.

Lea Michele

n
y
t
h
p o s s i b l e
n
g'
s

Unrequited

There's a tower
Where what remains of my heart is placed
Just never imagined you and I in unison
Would be the one to lock it away
But I guess it's okay
A series of choices made
Where fairytales no longer seize the day
And dragons and broken dreams need slayed
In such a daze
Created out of my own haze
With an outdated defense strategy
All a fantasy
A mystical army of one
That screams I'm someone's son
A world created after tasting your tongue
Such a bitter blade that won
Broke so much of me in just a day
Now I'm stuck in this land of yesterday
Because while I told myself I was strong
I found out I was wrong
So I scattered different pieces of my heart

Laid to rest the incorrect part
Tried not to cower as I climbed this tower
Mourning as I threw fragments of me out to sea
Because what's really left of me?
Simultaneously climbing
While somehow still drowning
Filled with all this doubting
A loss of words, always mouthing
Now I feel I've lost my calling
With a curse that's never calming
Feeling like it's the price I pay
For trying to be united
Unaware it was **unrequited**
Unaware that something had been ignited
The smallest flicker of flame inside
Almost unnoticeable
But whispers an eventual change in tide
That took with it the part of me I chose to hide
Realizing with wide eyes it survived
So deprived
Yet somehow still alive

Father

Your love was supposed to be a key
Ever present when I scraped a knee
And yet I still have people ask me
If I'd like to meet you
But what could I possibly have to learn
From a man who never took his turn
And though the child in me might still yearn
He's still healing from the burn

And at fifteen years old
"Confessions of a Broken Heart"
Tore me apart
And yet it was a song
I listened to for so long
Almost like a letter I never wrote you
Somehow a melody for just us two
Sung by another
Met with "oh brother"

I daydreamed, lost in rhyme
But every time
I dreamt of another you
Where the world was painted

In such a different hue
I was still left in a depressing shade of blue

So did you ever wonder what you left
Cause in your wake there was theft
Like in your absence you took with you
A part of me too
And yet
Each day the sun still set
And one day I'd bet
This would no longer be a threat

Words

There's something I need you to know
A side of me I've never shown
Out of fear you might not understand
And though it might sound absurd
I've always needed words
Never slurred
But always heard

And though I know you didn't mean to
Even right by my side
You left me
And what felt like emotional neglect
Left me feeling like a defect

You labeled me ungrateful
And truth be told I felt hateful
Because how could I
A child who didn't understand
The kind of pain that somehow felt planned
Give you
What I was never given

If I had gotten the words
And the validation that I needed
It would have changed everything
But those unsaid words
Left me feeling unheard
And something inside me stirred
In which I learned
To just study the birds
To hardly be seen or heard

A trauma not many understand
That leaves you with empty hands
Grasping for the love
Your inner critic has told you
You don't deserve
All because of words

Model Behavior

Flashback and it's 2010
Barely even men
And no one said when
Cause time and time again
My mind went back to you
But that was then
And this is now
So let me tell you how

A name on my list
Underlined in blue
Such a pretty hue
I thought so too
But this party isn't just for you
It's a gala for two
To convey what you put me through
And how I grew
Because something I never told you
Was that I was wearing my heart on my sleeve
And you were the first to leave
Yet you were the one who'd been chasing me

Confident as you were in your skin
You made my lack thereof into a crime
And you went on to pursue your dreams full-time
Leaving it all behind
But please don't stress
I'm no longer a mess
Hoping that this wasn't bad press
The past just alluded to model behavior I guess

Gold

Truth be told I was sold
To the lies you were able to mold
A relationship not on hold
Tucked in the fold
Non-disclosed
Right or wrong, no matter how bold
I wouldn't believe what I was told
A monster in disguise—so cold
I mistook you for gold

Now I've ripped off the blindfold
And instead of us growing old
I realize it was simply a story foretold
A lesson learned— though it felt like a scold
Left me out in the cold
With nothing but fools gold
I couldn't remold

Three Months

We met at a club
Filled with tigers and heat
Never expecting to meet
In the city of angels

So much happened in between
Like the fact that you were mean
And now I don't even remember
Was your favorite color green?

What I once thought was fate
That turned into a date
Is now insignificant

For three months too long
You played your favorite song
Somehow convincing me this was life-long
And when you said goodbye I wasn't strong
But believe me, I moved on

Because at one point I thought
I couldn't will a caterpillar to stay
And you were the butterfly that somehow got away
But believe me when I say that this isn't true today
And for the rest of your life you'll wish you had stayed

Blank Space

October 2014
Seeing your queen
Listening to Taylor set the scene
Not knowing I'd need a vaccine
For what I thought was a delicate cuisine
Because I began my chase
When I finally saw your face
Both in the same place
Mistaking a blank space
For grace
Later realizing the song set the pace
For games
And flames
With nothing but a name
On a list I'll never frame

Paint

Twenty-fifteen
Met through a screen
The furthest from mean
A handsome YouTuber
Made me wonder if we had a future
Without the need of a suture

And it wasn't the paint
That made me feel faint
But rather when you leaned in
Holding me close—it felt like a win
Almost a sin
A fresh coat—paper thin

Drinks in my city
A night not so pretty
But man were you witty
Just ask the committee

But with a secret so gritty
I felt compassion, not pity
And thought what we had was still pretty

Cried not because it was tricky
Or I didn't know how to behave
But because it was brave
And still somehow dug our grave

Narcissist

I've tried to start this a million times
Went and erased so many rhymes
Out of fear of you—of getting sued
Cause that's what a narcissist would do

But waiting in the wings, dear narcissist
Is this catharsis
Because it's finally time
To release myself from your ultimate crime

The triangulation
The emotional manipulation
Somehow fooled me into believing
That I was the one

Your gaslighting deceiving
My love so conceiving
Emotional warfare kept me weaving
And I never dreamt of leaving

But I gathered my courage
With my mind refurbished
And did what I could
The decision—so good
No longer questioning if I should

And truth be told
There's nothing to miss
But you'll still probably hiss
Mad if you read this
Cause we no longer kiss

Man I don't miss
That wretched Narcissist

The Fool

I wonder as I sit here at 5:30am
Airplanes flying overhead
Am I a fool
Or like The Fool?
Two very different things
A tarot card—not what you think
Reflecting on New York City in a blink

While there—so many questions left unsaid
So much spiraling inside my head
A kiss
So simple
So true
Yet why did it feel like there was something to lose?
A cause to confuse
Let's use it—a muse

But really, please don't fret
I'm happy we met
A trip I'll honestly never forget
Your name, your presence, in no way a threat

Not bitterly placed on this list of past rhymes
I promise I just had to free myself at the time
From my mind reeking havoc with crime
A low point I admit I've grown to despise
But I'm on my way up to clearer skies
I'll be back home soon—no battle cries
With a friendship I'm praying never cuts ties

What Love Is

I'VE ALWAYS BELIEVED in love. I grew up strongly believing in the kind of love that could conquer anything, but as an adult my views on love have shifted because of what it's put me through. Don't fret though. I'm not a cynic when it comes to love—just more realistic. My mind isn't clouded with an image of a quest filled with dragons and everything in between. Rather, my outlook on love has been shaped with a new knowledge that only comes with self-awareness. And within that knowledge is power, because with it I've discovered I never really knew what love is. This explains why I was always so adamant on handing over my power to people who couldn't care less about me. But I couldn't see it—putting myself in less than satisfactory situations because in my mind's eye I thought I had everything at the time. I was distracted though—refusing to see the true image of the person standing in front of me because I was too busy projecting. I let a fairytale version of love cloud my judgment and dull my senses. Because in the past I'd generally been pretty good at reading people, but when it came to love, I was left in the dark in more ways than one.

Being left in the dark changed my life. It opened me up to a realm of painful experiences I wish I could say I hadn't known before, but that were all too familiar. Love became a vice—something that somehow seemed both cursed and wicked. It caused me problems and strife. It made me feel like my lungs were filled with anything but life. But little did I know what I would learn from each and every one of these experiences—that despite the pain of each time my heart was broken, I would eventually come up for air in a sea of my own heartbreak. And out would spill something new—a deeper understanding of what wasn't there before. One being that self-love doesn't always have to be un-requited. In fact, it's required. But before I get too far ahead of myself, I should probably let the rest of this story unfold.

Things I Learned

"Your task is not to seek for love, but merely
to seek and find all the barriers within
yourself that you have built against it."

RUMI

1. Some of the nicest, most charming people can have the most toxic and shocking personalities behind closed doors.

2. Sometimes when the one that got away comes back, it isn't the fairytale you always imagined it would be.

3. Learning your love language is important because sometimes the way someone attempts to love you isn't the way you actually need to be loved.

4. Great sex doesn't always mean you're compatible.

5. Beware of the person who lacks empathy towards others because as much as you'd like them to, they won't develop it for you.

6. You're allowed to cut yourself free from emotional ties.

7. If a toxic person contacts you out of nowhere, they're more than likely trying to suck you back in. Don't fall for it.

8. The best revenge isn't a hot body because this implies that all you had to offer in the relationship was your body. You are worth more than what your body might have to offer.

9. The best revenge is success.

10. Communication is key. Always.

11. You shouldn't trust them if they're rude or belittle anyone working in customer service.

12. It's okay to mourn the loss of someone you thought was "the one." Just don't take up residency there for too long.

13. There's a difference between needing a little space and the silent treatment. One is healthy while the other, more often than not, is a manipulation tactic.

14. If we continue to repeatedly choose people who hurt us we may need to look within and find the reason we subconsciously continue to pick the wrong people time and time again.

15. There is nothing wrong with going to therapy.

16. If they use the nice things they do against you, chances are they aren't doing them with a pure heart or good intentions.

17. You have every right to want your feelings to be validated by your partner, but when validation is repeatedly not given to you, you will have to learn how to validate yourself. Sometimes this means learning how to do so on your own without them.

18. Sometimes we subconsciously seek a partner who might provide us with a happily ever after to a story from our own childhood. This partner is usually never good for us.

19. If they're bad for your mental health, they're bad for you.

20. You shouldn't be required to jump through rings of fire... no matter how much they claim to love you.

21. Sometimes "opposites attract" isn't true for everyone. And there's nothing wrong with that.

22. It's nice to know we're not alone in the fact that almost all of us have had moments where we look back and say, "What was I thinking?"

23. Emotional abuse is still abuse. Just because a scar can't be seen doesn't mean a wound isn't there, nor does it make it any less real.

24. We'll never forget our first love, but that doesn't mean we have to allow the memory of them to torture us.

25. There's nothing better than having a partner who wants to know which life experiences have helped shape you, and is patient with what and when you choose to share.

26. Some things start off fast, while others might start off slow. There is nothing wrong with either, but it's important to gauge and trust your instincts when it comes to finding what timing works for you.

27. If you catch them lying to you before you're officially together, then they'll continue to lie to you for the duration of your relationship. Save yourself the trouble and leave before then.

28. If they're consistently hot and then cold, contacting you a lot one second and ignoring you the next, then they're probably trying to keep you reeled in. Know your worth—walk away.

29. Love isn't a game. You should never have to compete for someone's affection.

30. The best apology isn't, "I'm Sorry." It's changing the behavior that warranted an apology in the first place.

31. If they apologize but continue the same behavior, they were never sorry to begin with.

32. You don't always meet the best people when you're inebriated.

33. Don't compare your relationship to that of others. You have no idea what goes on behind closed doors.

34. It's not always easy, but try not to rationalize being mistreated.

35. You are two separate people choosing to be together. You are not suddenly one entity.

36. Just because you lost yourself in the midst of someone else doesn't mean you can't find yourself again. Better yet, you might find somebody better and improved after what they've been through.

37. Sometimes there really is a good in goodbye.

38. You being an emotional person doesn't equate to a bad thing just because they're not.

39. Vulnerability in any relationship is important. Especially one that is romantic.

40. Learn to stand up for what you deserve and never placate bad behavior. When you allow this type of behavior, it only gives them permission to continue to mistreat you.

41. One day you will wake up and the weight of their presence will be gone.

42. You'll be okay. It might just take some time.

43. No relationship is worth the risk of losing hope for the future.

44. No one can complete you. You have everything you need to complete you already.

45. If you place all of your happiness in the hands of another, what happens if they leave?

46. There is nothing wrong with wanting to be a healthier, happier, or better version of you for your next relationship. Ground yourself in this positivity instead of revenge.

47. Effort will always be an attractive, required quality.

48. A healthy relationship has an almost even level of give and take.

49. Compromise and happy mediums make for better, healthier conflict resolutions.

50. Watch out for signs of gaslighting. Chances are you're not as crazy as your manipulator wants you to believe.

51. Past trauma is never an acceptable excuse for someone to emotionally or physically hurt you.

52. Some of the most fleeting moments spent with someone can somehow cause us the most pain.

53. Wishing for things to be different won't suddenly make them different.

54. Learn from your mistakes. They don't have to change you.

55. You are not defined by the mistakes people make when they hurt you.

56. Heartbreak is a knowledgeable journey—you just have to pay attention.

57. If you have to walk on eggshells over the most innocent, simple things, something isn't right.

58. Trust is one of the most important aspects of a romantic relationship.

59. If they don't want to build with you then they don't want to spend their life with you.

60. Don't compromise your life, your dreams, or your happiness for someone who has proven they aren't worthy of compromise. A real partner will never ask you to light yourself on fire just to keep them warm.

61. Don't forget about your friends just because you're in a relationship.

62. You'll probably mistake love for something completely different more than once.

63. "The past is in the past" is always a good mantra to live by.

64. "The past is in the past" includes past relationships *and* hook-ups.

65. Running into the arms of someone else because you're in pain won't make the pain go away.

66. Healing past wounds before something new isn't required, but sometimes it's easier to do on your own.

67. Be respectful on social media.

68. Emotional cheating is just as real as cheating itself.

69. Revenge sex can make for a fun story, but that's about it.

70. Sex might temporarily bury the emotions you don't want to feel, but they'll eventually resurface until you actually deal with them.

71. Finally dealing with your emotional baggage is a huge step in the right direction.

72. If you notice a smirk on their face when they say something rude to you then they get some kind of sick pleasure out of hurting you.

73. Run as fast as you can from people like #72.

74. There's nothing wrong with being excited about the potential of something new.

75. Just like there's nothing wrong with also being nervous about the potential of something new.

76. Set boundaries.

77. If they continuously overstep those boundaries with little to no remorse then it's time to figure out whether you need to find something new. Chances are you do.

78. There is no defined time period when you can or can't say I love you.

79. If you continuously find yourself saying, "I thought they were different", you're probably projecting a false image onto people rather than letting them show you who they are.

80. Just because you haven't been in an official relationship doesn't mean there's something wrong with you.

81. You can only do so much to try to get someone to lower the drawbridge to the walls around their heart. Eventually you have to move on if they don't let you in.

82. A hot body doesn't always mean an attractive personality.

83. "Hurt people hurt people..." is never a good enough excuse.

84. There's nothing wrong with leaving.

85. Realizing you deserve better is such a beautiful, yet bitter-sweet realization.

86. TV and movies don't accurately depict love.

87. You are allowed to be both a victim and a survivor simultaneously. There is power in owning both your story and truth.

88. Having too much on a victim mentality is never a good thing.

89. Sometimes we meet who we feel is the right person at the wrong time for a reason.

90. You don't have to take them back just because they realized what they had.

91. When you don't know your own worth, you invite others into your life who won't bother to learn it either.

91. You are always stronger than you think.

92. What you've been through does not define you.

93. You are not too damaged to deserve something good.

94. Despite how someone might have made you feel, you deserve the kind of love you've always dreamed of.

95. Your time is valuable. Don't let somebody else waste it.

96. Be upfront. There's no need to waste anybody else's time if you don't know what you want.

97. Double standards are never okay.

98. Conversations about whether you're exclusive or not shouldn't be avoided.

99. They can't read your mind, so speak up if you're not getting what you need.

100. If it feels like emotional warfare it probably is. And it isn't worth it.

101. We often want someone to be interested in us as well as our lives before we really show any interest in theirs. But they deserve effort and interest on our part too.

102. If they continuously disrupt your inner peace they might be doing it on purpose.

103. When you're triggered it's important to figure out why.

104. It's best to stop talking and take a breather when you're triggered rather than say something you'll later regret.

105. Just because someone can't learn to love you the way you deserve to be loved doesn't mean you can't learn to love yourself.

106. Arguments are natural, healthy even, but too much fighting isn't okay.

107. It's not your job to try to fix them.

108. Don't tunnel vision your focus so much on them that you forget to take care of yourself.

109. Sex doesn't always mean they'll stay.

110. If you know things have run their course, do the right thing and end it.

111. Don't lead someone on if you know you're not ready to get back out there yet.

112. It does no good to get even.

113. We don't always pick the right people when we don't know how to be okay on our own.

114. One partner can't do all the heavy lifting.

115. If dating is distracting you from something important it's okay to put it on the backburner.

116. Sometimes the decisions you're making are what's actually breaking your heart.

117. If they have no faith in your ability, the best satisfaction lies in doing it without them.

118. Fear from previous bad relationships can ruin the potential of something good.

119. No amount of money they make can buy you happiness together.

120. Sometimes things don't work out with someone because they're meant to work with someone else—someone better.

121. Don't lose years of your life dwelling in the pain they caused you.

122. You are in control of your thoughts—not the other way around.

123. If they never make time for you then they're not worth the wasted energy.

124. Don't become bitter, become better.

125. Neither partner should bring things to the table they know shouldn't be there.

126. Sometimes our memories like to play tricks on us by making us believe things were better than they actually were.

127. It's natural to feel lonely at times.

128. Learn to love yourself when you feel like no one else is willing to.

129. It's more than okay to date and get to know yourself.

130. Self-development is a key not everyone possesses. When you find it—use it.

131. Give yourself time to heal.

132. Let karma do its job while you're out living your best life.

133. Be careful of self-fulfilling prophecies.

134. Abandonment issues don't have to define you.

135. There's no need to creep on your ex's social media.

136. There's no guilt in giving away their things.

137. If they move on quickly... let them.

138. As much as you want to, there might not be a way to save their new partner from going through the same thing you did.

139. They can be both your biggest blessing and worst curse simultaneously.

140. Use them as an example of what not to look for next time.

141. They taught you what you don't deserve.

142. Sometimes we expect too much from someone who might be incapable of giving it to us.

143. The pain will help you grow if you let it.

144. What you see isn't always what you get.

145. The story we want isn't always the story that's written for us.

146. Sometimes someone isn't meant to continue on in our journey.

147. Wishing them bad harms you too.

148. Nobody else is going to save you.

149. Destroying someone because someone destroyed you creates an unnecessary and devastating cycle of destruction.

150. Crying is not a sign of weakness.

151. Just because they quit doesn't mean you have to quit on yourself too.

152. You're not hard to love.

153. Sometimes it really has nothing to do with you and everything to do with what they've been through.

154. Opening a window instead of sitting in the dark will improve your mood.

155. Honor how you feel when you feel it.

156. Heartache can feel weirdly alienating.

157. Love is not a light switch.

158. Listening to music can be healing, but it can also perpetually keep you entangled in the memories that cause you to relive pain.

159. Don't question what you deserve.

160. Both partners should have faith in each other.

161. If you can't believe them, why are you with them?

162. You should never have to beg someone to stay.

163. Saying, "I love you" with agony in your voice doesn't really sound like love when you think about it enough.

164. Despite what society might say or think, you're still a kid at twenty-three.

165. They should make you feel like they want to be with you.

166. You are the only person guaranteed to be in your life forever.

167. Over-thinking can ruin everything.

168. You can't always make someone understand you.

169. If they insult your insecurities they are not good for you.

170. Don't forget to also have goals outside of your relationship.

171. Sometimes they want you to pine over them. Don't give them that satisfaction.

172. You don't need to be perfect. You're allowed to make mistakes.

173. Leaving isn't mutually exclusive with giving up.

174. Asking yourself, "What if this is all there is?" is usually a sign that you're not only unhappy, but that you probably shouldn't stay.

175. Sometimes you just have to dance it out.

176. Don't convince yourself that no one cares about you.

177. True friends will be there through the heartache, but that doesn't mean you only have to talk about what you're going through.

178. It's okay to not want to live in what once was. Yesterday is gone.

179. They can touch your body, but make sure they can also touch your soul.

180. Don't let them turn your dream into a nightmare just because they don't understand it.

181. Avoid the gray area—where you're not really lovers, more than friends, but have no idea where you stand in each other's lives.

182. As you get older, you realize it's better to avoid the gray area at all costs.

183. Commitment is important if that's what you want.

184. If they wanted to make time for you they would.

185. Sometimes you have to ask yourself if they really have your best interest at heart.

186. Love will bloom again.

187. Holidays can still feel lonely while you're together.

188. Sometimes the best way to communicate everything you never had the opportunity to say is in a letter they'll never read.

189. There's nothing as deafening as complete silence on the ride home.

190. If they change the rules to the game every day, you're playing a game you'll never win.

191. Going to sleep angry next to each other is like going to sleep on two different sides of the same state.

192. They shouldn't want to shut you out each and every time.

193. There's always light in the dark somewhere.

194. Agreeing all the time is a fantasy, but at the end of the day they should still be on your side.

195. Pain can be channeled into inspiration, which in turn can be used to create.

196. Small doses of jealousy are healthy, but too much poisons everything.

197. What's inside their heart matters.

198. They can have everyone fooled—including you.

199. They don't get to be the one to decide they didn't hurt you.

200. Assuming they're giving someone else everything they never gave you will always be just a painful assumption.

201. Stop going back to the people who hurt you.

202. It can be like seeing color for the first time when you leave the world they only ever painted gray for you.

203. You can be both sad and beautiful at the same time.

204. The butterflies in your stomach distract your brain.

205. Whatever it might entail, let the last time be the last time.

206. You can give the right pieces of yourself to the wrong person.

207. You have value and worth, regardless of how other people treat you.

208. Having the same faith isn't required, but it is helpful.

209. Put to practice the phrase, "No one can make you feel inferior without your consent."

210. You shouldn't have to actively search for the good or compassion in someone.

211. As much as you believe in fantasy and fate, you can't turn back the hands of time.

212. Their lack of presence can feel like a ghost pulling at your heartstrings.

213. Your body is yours and yours alone.

214. Sometimes it feels like it's your heart versus common sense.

215. If you came to them empty handed would they still choose you?

216. Forgive them.

217. Forgive yourself too.

218. You might never get an apology.

219. The joy you're searching for is in you.

220. There's nothing better than vulnerability—than having someone let you in.

221. It's the little things that can make the biggest impact on your heart.

222. "Almost lovers" is such a weird, sad phrase when used to describe to someone.

223. Forgiveness isn't for them… it's for you.

224. They just can't walk in and out of your life like it's nothing.

225. Games are meant for fun, not for matters of the heart.

226. It's okay to admit you're not doing okay.

227. You shouldn't have to wonder which version of someone you'll get that day.

227. Don't feel stupid if you ignored the warning signs.

228. If your parents wouldn't approve of the way that they treat you, you probably shouldn't be with them.

229. Time seems to travels slowly when you're in the process of moving on.

230. You're probably right; you probably were the one real thing they'd ever know.

231. You'll never listen to certain songs the same way you did before them.

232. Sometimes you're exhausted not because of a lack of sleep but because of what they're putting you through.

233. Affirmations like, "I get better every day" are helpful and not as cheesy as they seem.

234. Love is work, yes, but it's also supposed to be easy.

235. It's not an end. It's just an ending.

236. As much as you think they might, other people can't feel the love you have radiating inside for them.

237. When someone treats you in a way you're not used to being treated, it can feel foreign; but it doesn't mean you have to reject being treated with kindness.

238. They'll never look deceitful in their childhood photos.

239. Real love can take you higher than what you've experienced before.

240. You attract better people by being yourself.

241. One day you might notice you still sleep on the same side of the bed, but this discovery doesn't have to mean anything more than that.

242. No matter how much they want you to, you can't magically change. And chances are you shouldn't have to.

243. Never convince yourself that you're not good enough for something good.

244. If sorrow was like electricity, then heartache would have enough charge to light an entire city.

245. You might not know you're being abused.

246. You can practically drown yourself in alcohol and still not forget.

247. You don't have to give someone a second chance if you don't want to.

248. You'll go the wrong direction if you're holding onto things you're meant to let go of.

249. No answer is an answer in and of itself.

250. You'll remember the plans that never got a chance to happen.

251. Educate yourself on the warning signs to look out for next time.

252. You can't always expect someone to dream like you do.

253. Don't dim your light just so they can think they shine.

254. The universe will continue to provide you with similar situations until you learn the lesson it's trying to teach you.

255. Don't kill yourself fighting for someone who wouldn't fight for you.

256. Being selfish doesn't always need to have a negative connotation.

257. Trust the timing of your life. Things happen when they're supposed to.

258. Show them they should have never doubted you.

259. They aren't good for your mental health if they're giving you a panic attack.

260. Don't turn into someone you don't recognize.

261. It's not wrong to feel as deeply as you do.

262. Having your friends tell you that they're such a great person, when they're not, is not a good enough reason to stay.

263. If they cheated in the past they'll probably cheat on you—unless they've learned their lesson.

264. Believe it or not, binge watching a TV show can actually be quite therapeutic.

265. There's nothing wrong with wanting to be wanted, but don't let this desire lead you into the arms of the wrong person.

266. Running away because you're terrified that they'll leave you first only leaves them with a scar similar to one someone left you.

267. Resistance to what is, is what causes us pain.

268. All the hook ups in the world won't drown out the noise—won't silence the scream of your pain.

269. You'll convince yourself that you'll always remember what you should have said or done differently... until one day it no longer crosses your mind anymore.

270. Being loyal before you need to be isn't the problem, not disclosing it is.

271. Don't let anyone make you feel guilty for feeling things on a deeper level than they're able to comprehend.

272. Shouldn't they want to understand what's going on inside your head?

273. You are not a canvas for their projected pain.

274. Narcissists only respond to consequences. Something like, "Get your shit together or leave..."

275. You can help them paint their father's house and they'll still stop talking to you.

276. A surefire sign of being with the wrong person is feeling drained.

277. You are more than enough.

278. Secrets may not make friends, but they also have the ability to ruin relationships.

279. If you constantly affirm that they'll leave why are you so surprised when they do?

280. "Oh" always means so much more than people think it does.

281. You'll be unsure if you can ever be called the same nickname again. Chances are the answer is no.

282. The best hook ups are the ones in which neither of you belong to the other but you're still able to share in intimate moments together.

283. There's nothing worse than a bad sexual experience because you didn't ask for what you want.

284. If they leave shortly after they cum they probably don't love you.

285. It's probably best to not hook up with someone you have history with unless you know it's nothing more than sex and old feelings won't bubble to the surface again.

286. It's not selfish to leave.

287. You are not a bad person for making a mistake.

288. The best thing you can get back is yourself.

289. You don't have to disclose everything from your past right away. Take your time.

290. Arguing over the phone will never not be stupid.

291. Every time they reach out you don't have to reply.

292. Talking about what could have been will almost always lead to tears.

293. Sometimes you'll still know exactly where they'll be when you glance at the time.

294. Details you used to remember eventually fade.

295. Somehow, somewhere, you'll come across a stranger that smells just like them—flooding your senses and thoughts with memories you had no idea were still there.

296. Books are a form of therapy.

297. Thoughts, feelings, and words can and will get lost in translation.

298. Love is _____. *Write your own personal definition in the space provided. I believe that love is a spiritual development between two people who choose to be together.

299. Emotional manipulation is a type of abuse.

300. The idea of falling in love is a myth because, when you think about it, falling means you have to get back up.

301. If you claim they stole your happiness there's a very good chance you weren't happy in the first place.

302. If they're not passionate about anything, they're either incredibly boring or too afraid to admit what their passion really is.

303. Watch what their eyes light up for. Is it ever you?

304. Living in a different city can still somehow feel like long distance.

305. Love bombing is an abusive, covert technique abusers use to make you stay.

306. Take responsibility for your feelings rather than place blame. Instead of, "You make me feel desperate" flip the script by saying, "I feel desperate around you."

307. Knowing the definition of triangulation in relation to narcissistic abuse can be a powerful game changer.

308. There is no relationship without trust.

309. No matter what stage the relationship is in - whether you've just started dating or you've been together for a while - if you wouldn't want them to talk to someone inappropriately, then why would you?

310. The best way to get a narcissist to leave you is to pretend you've suddenly become boring.

311. A narcissist feeds off your reactions, which is why they provoke you for a response.

312. When you outgrow defense mechanisms they will suddenly do more harm than good.

313. Looking for the good in someone isn't a negative quality until you realize you've dated one too many monsters in disguise.

314. Love isn't the only thing you should be seeking.

315. Stop the self-blame.

316. Their most attractive quality should be how they treat other people—including you.

317. If you've had a parent leave or be absent from your life it only increases, not damages, your capacity to love.

318. Don't make costly mistakes just to feel something again.

319. Always continue to believe in magic. This is a quality not everyone can possess.

320. Soulmates don't always have to be romantic.

321. If you continue to affirm that men or women are trash, don't be surprised when it's all that shows up.

322. It's a double standard when your friend can date someone from your past, but gets mad when you date someone from his or hers.

323. The opposite of love is _____. *Write your own personal definition in the space provided. I believe that the opposite of love is laziness.

324. There's never not a time to listen to Taylor Swift's "We Are Never Ever Getting Back Together" when you're going through a breakup.

325. Fulfillment whispers lies that say, "Once you find a relationship you'll be happy."

326. When we identify with our mind we get caught up in believing that our identity stems from not only our thoughts, but also our pain.

327. Let go of the fear that if you are your true, authentic self someone, will leave you.

328. Ask yourself if you self-sabotage because somewhere deep down, you don't believe you deserve good things.

329. There's so much more to life than being in a relationship.

330. If you blame your optimism you might end up losing it.

331. One day you'll realize that all those sad songs no longer hold any power over you.

332. Your identity does not stem from the way that you think.

333. Don't build a wall between you and your willingness to be vulnerable.

334. If the hands of fate have dealt you some less than favorable cards, you're allowed to discard them.

335. There's nothing wrong with going after what you want—just make sure it isn't harmful to you.

336. Someday you'll be in the exact same place you made memories with someone, but it doesn't have to negatively affect you.

337. Don't forget about your dreams just because they're focused on theirs. You're both allowed to accomplish different things simultaneously.

338. You should both know better than to put yourselves into a type of situation you know you shouldn't be in.

339. The best way to help them see your point of view in an argument, as well as the flaws in their logic, is by asking them a question.

340. The ending often spoils what was once a beautiful beginning, but that doesn't mean it has to.

341. Stop wondering if they ever think about you.

342. They say that true love's kiss can break any curse, but what if you're kissing the villain in the story?

343. Crying in your car becomes a normal thing if you don't want anyone else to see.

344. Despite it sometimes being hard to find, there's still so much to be grateful for.

345. You could probably write an entire book on what you've been through.

346. Visualizing negative outcomes only causes more negativity in your life.

347. It's okay if you don't want to live a traditional life.

348. If you don't like the page of the story you're on, it might be because you haven't learned what you need to bring that chapter to a close.

349. Sobbing in your mother's arms, though it might be incredibly awkward at the time, feels like coming home.

350. Stop choosing people who don't choose you.

351. Abusive relationships aren't mutually exclusive with physical abuse.

352. How they treat their animals says a lot about them.

353. There is healing in tears.

354. Console your inner child when they're hurting.

355. Life isn't happening on the ground so stop looking down and hold your head up high.

356. Block them if you need to.

357. Your future self will thank you if you take care of yourself now.

358. Don't miss out on what's in front of you because of what you've left behind.

359. Breathe.

360. Stop telling yourself you have to put on an act. You don't have to get good at pretending you're okay.

361. The now dead flowers they once gave you can be a reminder as to why you'll never go back to them.

362. If you ever listen to it again, the song you envisioned dancing to at your wedding will never be the same.

363. It's incredibly powerful to speak up after being silenced for so long.

364. Learn to be okay on your own.

365. Continuous self-pity is a never-ending trap of the mind.

366. Change your mind… change your life.

367. They were right when they said not every person you lose is a loss.

368. Listen to your gut instinct if it's telling you something isn't right.

369. Let someone some show you who they are before you assume.

370. Awareness is key.

371. If you create boundaries it's probably best to follow through with them.

372. Learning how to casually date might bring forth a new awareness as to why you always dive into new romance headfirst.

373. The only person you should change for is you.

374. Emotional neglect and abandonment can cause Complex PTSD, which will undeniably affect interpersonal relationships in the future. So not everything you're going through in your relationships may be your fault. It may be in result of past trauma.

375. Knowledge is power. Educate yourself on why you might do the things you do.

376. Don't fall prey to the social stigma of things that can have a positive affect in your life. IE: self-help and therapy.

377. Your inner-critic will tell you nothing but lies.

378. You can unlearn behavior you were once forced to learn to feel safe.

379. Realizing that walking away from someone was the best thing you could have done for yourself is incredibly validating.

380. If they're making you question your reality, they might be the one that's crazy—not you.

381. Though your heart might be in the right place it might also be causing you to not think straight.

382. Toxic masculinity has got to go.

383. It's okay to stand out—to be seen.

384. Withholding small truths because you think they'll judge or leave you will cause more problems than you think.

385. Don't give up opportunities in your life just because you're focused on the wrong things.

386. It'll take some time to be you again—to fully heal.

387. Somewhere out there, someone feels the same way about love that you do.

388. You are not crazy.

389. Being alone isn't the worst thing you can be.

390. Someday you'll understand why you had to go through everything you've been through.

391. Just because they give you attention doesn't mean they deserve your affection.

392. Your mental health is important.

393. The pain they caused you says more about them than it does about you.

394. You don't have to hold onto old memories if you don't want to.

395. Loving the wrong person isn't a romantic death sentence.

396. Having a New Year's kiss isn't as magical as it seems.

397. There is nothing wrong in fighting for what you deserve.

398. What you once perceived as weakness is actually your greatest strength.

399. You'll never regret devoting yourself to the kind of self-love and healing you've always needed.

400. They say the greatest thing you'll learn is to love and be loved in return, but you might learn more about yourself when it's unrequited.

Bitter

YOU CAN EITHER let every bad romantic situation you've been through, or are going to go through, make you bitter or make you better. One will continue to drag you down—forcing you down a dark and twisty road that only leads to more heartache and bad decisions. On the other hand, the other leads to empowerment—with the kind of healing that awakens such a self-awareness that it gives you the kind of control you need to not just survive, but thrive. One is driven by negative emotions, while the other helps you realize that your emotions don't control you but rather you are in control of your emotions. Which will you choose?

Leaving You

LEAVING YOU WAS the beginning of something new. It marked the end of a chapter—that chapter being you. But it also marked the beginning of a journey—a journey in loving myself like both of us never did. So I did what I had to do—I walked away from the emotional abuse, the lies, and the fights. And it was like coming up for air. It was almost like my whole life I'd lived in a bubble under the sea. So, as I washed upon the shore, it was territory I had never explored, which only forced me to expand and grow into the parts of myself I'd never known before. But that doesn't mean it was always easy. Loving myself, in a way, almost felt like it came with consequences. It forced me to delve further into the darker parts of myself than I ever had before—reflecting on what caused me to be this way in the first place. It was a beautiful, bittersweet feeling. On one hand I felt free, and on the other I felt the weight of every burdening and hateful thing I'd been carrying with me under the uncharted seas of my own creation. And to be honest, sometimes it feels like I'm still drowning, as though I'm being swept underneath a familiar current again—one that leaves me feeling weak in its wake before I realize that my hand is just below the surface. I can see the light shining through—can feel myself about to break the surface of the water again. And yet it never makes, nor ever made, that first breath of fresh air not string. Because though it's easier to visit where you've been rather than stay, it still hurts to see the ruins of the kind of person you once were.

Patience

IT'S IMPORTANT TO remember to have patience with yourself, with your feelings, and with your triggers. Though self-development and self-awareness are crucial, they aren't always easy. Sometimes things in our lives have affected us in drastic, unconscious ways. Unaware that they've affected us so much, we're often confused as to why we react as strongly as we do to certain situations. This is why patience is mandatory and why being kind to ourselves while we work through the things we know we're better off without is necessary—especially if we're going to attempt to work on both the recovery and healing process simultaneously.

Without patience, we can't move forward. Without it we stay stuck—only increasing the negative voices in our heads that tell us we're nothing more than what we've been through. But when we're patient and when we're kind, we realize that this state of mind is a lie—that our identity does not stem from these things and that no matter how much misfortune we have received we still have the ability to find the light in the darkness. So as you gather your courage to move on, to heal any type of physical or emotional wound, be patient. Healing doesn't happen overnight, but you'd be surprised at just how much healing can occur when you practice both patience and kindness with yourself during this period of your life.

Therapy

IF YOU FEEL like you could benefit from therapy—utilize it. These people are trained, educated professionals for a reason. They're here to help us make sense of the things we can't always make sense of on our own. It doesn't matter why you feel like you might need to go—whether it's because of the past, the present, something traumatic you've been through, or because you're looking for clarification to questions and answers you've never been able to make sense of. These questions could involve love—like why you continue to choose the wrong person time and time again. No matter the subject, a therapist is there to help you find an answer.

Even the healthiest people can benefit from therapy. So those of us who feel as though we might need a little extra help have nothing to feel scared or ashamed of. There's nothing wrong with needing or wanting to go to therapy. In fact, it's brave to stand up in a world that often sits down when it comes to social stigmas. So don't be afraid to stand up for what you need to do. Don't be afraid to face your fears in order to be the best version of you. Because at some point you will inevitably have to face these fears, and therapy will help put you in the right frame of mind when you do.

The Museum of Broken Relationships

———⌒———

Name of donor: Andrew Kendall

Object/Exhibit: Two unworn "I'll Be Your Mickey" Disneyland tees.

Description/Story:
FLASHBACK AND IT'S the summer of 2015. Can you remember it—feel it? I can. There's a warm breeze, a signal of some sort of new beginning, and a smile on my face that I only now realize never felt right. It was a summer of firsts—of feeling ready, of movie-like moments, and diving headfirst into something so unexpectedly beautiful at the time that I couldn't help but feel hopeful. There's a certain level of unexpectedness in these moments though—a certain kind of awareness you miss simply because instead of letting that person reveal who they are, you assume. My assumptions led to a disaster that almost destroyed me, but before I get too far let me set the scene.

We had met briefly in the beginning of the year, but neither of us would give a second thought toward the other until much later. Our first date was four months later and to be honest (as

I type this) I haven't been on a date since. It was a date to remember. The kind of date that makes you forget your cell phone is in your pocket and is filled with so much laughter and good conversation that it doesn't even matter. He was headstrong, driven, and nothing and no one would penetrate the armor he had formed to get what he wanted out of life. And just like that, captivation reeled me in.

Pressing fast forward through moments like a midnight snack, cute texts with detailed plans for the future, and secretly buying two couple tees from Downtown Disney the night before we'd make it official and it wouldn't be long until those watching would begin to notice those amazing feelings slowly fade. Except he was very good at hiding it. Sadly I was too, but there was a drastic difference: I often wore my heart on my sleeve and he was a narcissist. Eventually everything that initially attracted him to me, everything that he seemed to adore, suddenly became everything that made me bad in his eyes. At times it felt like he would look at me with such hate—often provoking me with emotional abuse so that when I reacted, I was the one who looked crazy.

Fast-forward just one more time and, though we had detailed plans for the future, I left. And all I was left with were two unworn couple tees and the kind of scars people don't understand just because they can't be seen—because he didn't hit me. But he may as well have. Each time I had to face the emotional abuse, it felt as though I was being choked—slowly suffocating at the hands of a heartless soul who only wanted me in his life for the sick pleasure of torturing.

Different

IF YOU FIND yourself saying, "I thought they were different" time and time again, chances are it isn't them... it's you. While it's natural to experience this once in awhile, it isn't normal to experience this every time you attempt a new relationship. If this is something that continuously happens, then it's likely that your expectations are getting in the way and are in turn projecting an image onto who *you* want this person to be rather than who they are. And oftentimes this is exactly how awful people slip in between the cracks and find their way into warm, welcoming arms.

Responsibility

THERE'S A CERTAIN degree to which things are truly not our fault, but if we cannot learn to take responsibility for our actions we will only continue to be a victim. And allowing ourselves to stay in this mindset does nothing for us—often keeping us stagnant in a frame of mind that only causes us more problems. It's not about blaming ourselves, though. More often than not we, the victim, are not to blame. This is why it's important to take responsibility for our actions when we begin to notice that we put ourselves in the same situations time and time again—the situations where we ignore the warning signs, when we desperately seek out the wrong companions because we're lonely, or when we don't work on a kind of self-awareness that could actually solve these kind of problems. This is when we perpetually become a victim—entrapping ourselves in an endless cycle of victimhood because we're too scared to eradicate the voice in our head that tells us we're undeserving of good. In result, we fall victim to both our internal and external circumstance, unable to take responsibility for the choices we made that got us here. But life doesn't have to be that way. When we learn to take responsibility for our actions, to stop putting blame where it doesn't belong when it doesn't belong there, a world of opportunity opens up for us and life suddenly becomes our own.

A Conversation

───────

To PROTECT AN identity and to make this more fun, we'll call the person I'm talking to about my current funk, guys, and relationships... New York.

Me: I guess I just feel like so much is going on in my mind right now and I don't really know why. I've been through a lot that's really affected my outlook on love... and that's the root of what I'm trying to work through and get closure from. I guess sometimes, though, some part of me feels like I opened up this can of worms and that I did this to myself. But really all I want to do is heal.

New York: I feel you. I have been through so much and the longer I've been single the more I worry about love honestly.

Me: There's honestly no one here I'm interested in dating.

New York: That's exactly how I feel here. I always say in my head, "No offense, but can at least one person impress me?"

Me to me Move to California

Me: Boo to the men in New York if they can't impress you.

Me: Guys here, for me at least, bore me. They're either jerks or still want to party—creating a lens over their life that tries to filter out giving a fuck. While I'm over here like nah, it's time to start giving a fuck. Like sure, have fun, but don't people want to also have fun LATER in life—settle down, and maybe even retire early because their ambition got them to the place where they could afford to? I want to build a life, not something temporary where whoever I'm with wants something totally different. I'm just ready for someone who *is* different. Who knows their self-worth but also respects mine. I want someone to really build something with. Building is important but nobody ever wants to put in that effort so I stay alone until I can find someone who's ready and willing to.

Me to me *Where did you go? What are you thinking?*

Sometimes it feels like I'm the only one of who paints a picture of this dream.

But someone, somewhere, will have the perfect paint for this canvas made for two. I just have to be patient because someday I'll look up and everything will be different

The Next day:

New York: I totally get what you mean. I think I'm a specific type of person and I don't just shack up with anyone so who I spend time with is an important investment to me. Nobody really views relationships like that and so many people get caught up on an idea of who they think you are versus who you actually are. Or someone has such an idea of what a relationship is supposed to be like versus allowing it to be organic and natural. Most don't understand the dynamic I'm looking for overnight and I totally get that and am willing to work for it if it's mutual, it just never is.

Me: So the wedding will be in 2019, right? No, but all-joking aside I understand that. I guess sometimes for me it just feels like love is sort of one of the last areas in my life I need to work on and self-develop. I've worked very hard over the last year and a half to shape my life into what it is, but love still feels like that one place I know I need growth because of everything I've been through. For years I made the mistake of giving some of the best parts of myself to the wrong people. I watched as my idea of love slowly began to fade and for some reason I convinced myself to endure the pain these people caused—only further convincing myself that was what love is. I still very much believe in love and though I know it's not supposed to be all sunshine and daises I think we're supposed to wait for that person that things not only fully click with, but who doesn't make us feel difficult to love. Who makes us realize and say things like, "Wow… after all this time this is what it's supposed to be like."

New York: I believe I'll feel it when it's real or when it's something to fight for. Honestly haven't felt that way in so long, which is where my current apprehension comes from I guess. But then I'm reminded that love like that shouldn't come often.

Me to me Like I said, move to California

Sometimes our thoughts have the ability to feel alienating because of what we've been through. But after this conversation I realize I'm not so alone in this way of thinking after all. And it's one of the most refreshing feelings in the world—even if the only thing that comes from it is not feeling so alone.

Something My Therapist Told Me

———————⌒———————

"LOOK AT IT like this: It's almost like PTSD. You're on a cliff looking down on a beach where you experienced a shark attack and you're afraid of even standing on the beach again let alone getting in the water. But here's the thing… you don't have to jump right back in. It's natural, normal even, to fear another attack, but eventually you're going to have to dip your toes back in the water. Especially if you want to find what you're looking for."

A Feeling

Flashback
And suddenly you're back
But not "you" as in a person
More so a place
In a different time and space

And suddenly I'm visiting
An old, yet familiar face
An older version of me
Something I've worked very hard not to be

It's comforting knowing that this feeling won't stay
That sometime soon I'll return back to May
To be able to say things as simple as hey
Without masking that I'm not doing okay

One more thing before I go
It feels like I've taken a blow
Harsh and unexpected
Lonely and dejected
Almost hollow inside

With nowhere to hide
A feeling I hate each and every time.

I DON'T WANT to offer any type of explanations, at least written, for the poems in this book because I truly believe that the beauty of both art and poetry is up for interpretation. But I wanted to comment on something I experienced while writing it. I wrote A Feeling in the midst of what Pete Walker, in his book *Complex PTSD: From Surviving to Thriving*, would call a flashback. Walker writes that, "Survivors of traumatizing abandonment are extremely susceptibility to painful emotional flashbacks, which unlike ptsd do not typically have a visual component." He adds that, "These feeling states can include overwhelming fear, shame, alienation, rage, grief and depression. They also include unnecessary triggering of our fight/flight instincts."

In the midst of this flashback, I found myself lost to a voice inside my head that I thought I had long forgotten. I felt as though, in the process of working through the pain of my past experiences, I had opened up a floodgate of feelings I wasn't prepared for. It felt like everything around me began to collapse. I entered into what felt like an old, yet familiar world and in result I began to overthink everything—even the most simplistic of things. In a way I felt like I was going crazy.

The mind is a powerful thing and I'm honestly not sure that I will ever understand what lasted around the span of four days, in which there was so much going on in my brain that it physically hurt. What was weird was that there was never really an image in particular that haunted me. It was a question, or rather a cluster of questions: Am I ever going to be able to move on from the things, from the trauma, and the people in my life that have negatively affected my relationships and ability to love? And what the hell is going on with me?

I don't know if I'll ever really know the answer to that last question. But I do know what helped—telling myself, "You are not the pain other people have caused you. You are not their mistakes. You will healthily work through these things like you have everything else in your life. Relax. Just breathe and have faith."

Forgiveness

I'm learning to let the space
Between where I'm at
And where I want to be
Heal me
Instead of throw me back out to sea
Cause forgiveness it seems
Has to start with me
And work its way around
Like a crown
That will never again let me down

A Few Corrections

IN MY FIRST book, *The Dark Dictionary*, I wrote about a relationship as it unfolded. I'm able to revisit particular events—like what was a wonderful, yet still simple, first date. I also explained why I left—claiming I needed to be selfish while I wrote my book, but failing to include why. That why, I've come to find, is important. What was missed the first time around was a knowledge as to why our relationship quickly turned sour. Though at one point in time what I wrote rang true, that isn't the case anymore. Being left in the dark filtered out the truth and by the time that filter had been lifted, I felt it was too late to change my words. What I wrote at the time was authentic and changing it felt like it would alter that. I needed time to process, but I also needed time to cool down. I was mad that I was oblivious to what was going on right in front of me for as long as it did. I was being emotionally abused—made to believe I was at fault for everything he put me through. So as both a victim and a survivor, I'm here to take back the power that was stolen from me by making a few corrections. Because with new knowledge comes new power, and with both he no longer possesses the ability to manipulate my reality into an emotional rollercoaster of abuse—severing the sick, psychotic need he felt he had to put me through in order to feel good about himself.

While some might ask, "How on earth did you not know you were being abused?" with a stupid look on their face, I only have this to say: There is so much to emotional abuse that you don't see. Like the fact that there are forces at work in your mind that help mask the fact that you're being abused in the first place. Something called trauma bonding linked me to my abuser, which created such an emotional attachment between my abuser and myself that I was convinced that the emotional warfare was nothing more than typical arguments couples went through. That in turn led me to question my reality—a technique called gaslighting, which abusers use to convince you that it's all in your head because they want to make you feel crazy when you react. They want you to feel crazy, because if you fall for this technique, chances are you'll blame yourself—not second-guessing the abuse.

In my life I am lucky enough to have learned what was going on and had the ability to leave, but that doesn't make what happened any less harmful. But here on this page, is where I take my power back.

Corrections:

"A week after my friend's gorgeous wedding, I met someone who will have forever changed my life. The date was simple, but it was one for the record books. It was one filled with the hope of a new beginning. There were smiles and laughter, and I hung on to almost every word. It was one of those dates where you lose all track of time, where neither party even glances at their phone, which is sadly rare nowadays. To me, that meant something. It was the beginning of my first relationship, one I will treasure and keep with me for the rest of my life."

Though it's true that I will keep parts of this relationship with me for the rest of my life, it's not for the reasons I originally wrote. My life *was* forever changed, but not because I found someone amazing. Rather it was because I found the opposite. I found someone who pretended to care—especially in front of other people. There are meaningful moments I will never forget, yes, but overall this relationship taught me exactly what I don't deserve and that, because I didn't know my self-worth, I let someone into my life who treated me accordingly—if not less than. But everything happens for a reason and this entire, crazy experience was a lesson on abuse—about how to better look out for warning signs. And next time I see the signs, I'll hopefully have enough common sense to leave early this time.

> *"I was in my first long-term relationship, but because of past issues I had never dealt with, I was creating problems within it. Believe me when I say that though it may not have been fun for my partner, I can guarantee it felt worse for me. I was dealing with things in my head that I didn't quite understand, which to me felt far worse and frustrating."*

This quote is bittersweet because, though it's true that I had issues in my past I hadn't worked through, it was used to my abusers advantage. I was made out to be crazy—basically told in both words and actions that I wasn't good enough and that if I didn't change I would be abandoned. So I felt guilty, as though the burdens of what I went through were ruining what was right in front of me—something I had convinced myself of so many times in the past. This fueled me. I was determined to not let history repeat itself. No matter how unaware I was of what was actually going on. But reading this quote in the present makes me feel like our "love" was some type of sick game to be won.

"Real estate was sadly a venture that didn't fit into my picture and was a decision I had made for all the wrong reasons."

The wrong reasons can be summed up in two words: my relationship. He hated my creativity. He wanted to be with someone with a "real job" so he tried to snuff out my creativity like a light. But love is not a light switch. It's safe to say that I carried on and did exactly what he didn't want.

"Further down the line I began to feel a chapter that wasn't in my book was coming to a close, and that chapter was my relationship. It wasn't something spur of the moment I decided, but rather it was a decision that took a few weeks to carefully reflect on to make sure I was making the correct move. So a few weeks shy of a year, I made a selfish decision to end what I felt was no longer working."

Thank God this chapter came to a close. But the craziest part of this quote is how much I remember those few weeks it took to reflect on what I knew I needed to do. I was scared—terrified that I might make the wrong decision. Sadly, what I had was all I had known. I didn't know any better partially because I was also unaware of the abuse at the time. So though I was emotionally and physically exhausted from everything I was going through, I simply convinced myself that I needed to be selfish. My first book became my scapegoat, but what I also knew was that I wouldn't have been allowed to take the time I needed to write. What I desperately needed to get away from were the irrational arguments and accusations that consumed me. Because if I had asked for the time that I needed to get work done I would have been accused of doing things I'd never do—something that happened so often that I stopped being shocked by it. In turn I realized that my "partner" didn't know me and that he probably never would. He didn't care. I was just some plaything to torture— nothing more. So I used my dreams as an excuse, which in turn actually worked out in my favor because I accomplished a decent amount of them. But I knew I couldn't focus on what I needed to accomplish while we were together. I would have been too worried about him, about us, about what type of argument we would repeatedly get into. Hence why this quote isn't wrong about this chapter of my life that needed to be closed, but it definitely wasn't as selfish of a decision as I had made it out to be. I needed to do what I had never done and that was look out for me.

"I have nothing against my ex, nor do I wish him any harm in the world. In fact, I only hope for the opposite. I wish him all the love in the world because he was the catalyst I always knew I needed but was never truly prepared for. And it is my hope that we both propelled each other forward in the next stages of our lives alone."

This is still true. I harbor no resentment against my ex despite the fact that I no longer put him up on a pedestal. So though some might take this chapter as a hostile attempt to get revenge, I really don't see it as such. I see it more so as a then and now kind of a chapter simply because I know that I was the best damn thing to ever happen to him, but I was also naïve and uneducated on narcissism at the time. I was young and believed that if I tried to love someone with every part of my being that there was no way I could be abused. I was wrong, and from that came the greatest lesson God has ever given me to learn. And though he's bitter that I left, because all abusers are, I know that he propelled me forward to exactly where I needed to be. Because if you're paying close enough attention you realize that the abuse backfired. I didn't let it bury me like he planned. I let it fuel me forward—realizing that I wasn't crazy and that the best revenge is moving on without resentment. Oh, and also success.

"I knew just how much I was giving up to gain something else, something that, though it felt hard to do, was still very important to me, and despite my final decision, it still broke my heart just as much."

I gave up abuse to gain freedom. I just didn't know it at the time. So though it broke my heart to leave, I also felt a huge weight miraculously vanish from my shoulders.

"Despite the unraveling of one thing, I began to put myself together more and more as the time between our breakup and where I'm at now passed."

This one isn't wrong. I wanted to include it because it's an important reminder that just because one thing falls apart doesn't mean everything else can't come together around it in a way that becomes both beautiful and healing.

Gaslighting

ONCE YOU'VE BEEN fooled you think you know every trick in the book—somehow believing that nothing can sneak up on you or take you for granted anymore. But this isn't always the case. When they say expect the unexpected, believe them because covert types of abuse have a way of sneaking up on you. Without knowing the warning signs of gaslighting it can somehow fall into a blind spot—silently smothering your story while your abuser pretends they have no idea what they're doing.

Gaslighting is a form of emotional abuse—a manipulative technique that often makes you question not only your reality, but also your sanity. It's trauma inducing. The manipulator often provokes their subject so much that when they finally react they accuse them of being over the top—of being crazy for having reacted in the first place. Why? Because if they convince you that you're crazy their abuse slips under the radar. They can continue to abuse you.

They purposely lie about situations so they can hit you back with, "I have no idea what you're talking about" even if you have proof. It's deceiving. You begin to question not the validity of your relationship, but rather the quality of your own thoughts. You begin to wonder things like: Am I crazy? Or what's wrong with *me*? But it's important to trust your gut instinct. If it's telling you it's not you, chances are it's telling you the truth.

Was I Crazy?

Was I crazy when you would deliberately cause an argument just to get a reaction?

Was I crazy when you would lie and make up an entire situation just to see if I would be jealous?

Was I crazy when you would try to blame everything on me and take zero responsibility for your actions?

Was I crazy when I confided in you the things that I've been through and you used those exact same things against me?

Was I crazy when you tried to convince *me* that I somehow used to be in love with people who had only ever been acquaintances?

Was I crazy when I left and the only real reason you hated me was because if you had known you would have had time to leave me first?

No. I wasn't crazy. You were—as well as unkind, selfish, and narcissistic behind closed doors. You only wanted me to believe I was crazy for your own manipulative game, but your plan backfired when I put myself in therapy and realized it wasn't me… it was you.

Why Do We Stay?

WHY DO WE stay when we know what we're in isn't right for us? Why do we stay when somewhere in the future, waiting in the wings, is someone that will give us everything we've ever dreamed of—everything that the person in front of us would rather leave for dead? Maybe we tell ourselves that this isn't true. Maybe we've convinced ourselves that this is all there is—that there couldn't possibly be anything better than this. Something new feels terrifying. But the truth lies in discovering that the relationship draining the life out of us is the fallacy—not finding something new. Yet we convince ourselves that we somehow don't deserve better. We tell ourselves that this is all that's in store for us. We do this by scaring ourselves—by telling ourselves that because this is all we've ever known, it's all we're ever going to know. Starting over doesn't feel like an option. But starting over is the key we've been missing. With it we're finally able to take a step forward, to find ourselves again, and acknowledge that we didn't deserve what they put us through. So why do we stay, when the fact that we even have to ask ourselves this question should be reason enough not to?

Reopen Old Wounds

RATHER THAN REOPEN old wounds—sometimes the one that got away is better off staying that way. Because there's no guarantee that things will pan out the way we've envisioned them and when they don't we've only caused ourselves to experience the same pain twice.

History

⸻

EVERYONE HAS A history—a story to tell about what they've been through. In result, most of us usually have baggage. Because let's face it... we've all been through something. What most of us forget though is that these things do not define us. Our history is just evidence of where we've been—not where we've been forced to take up residency.

We usually expect others to be accepting and patient of the not-so-pleasant things we bring to the table, while not offering the same courtesy in return. We're quick to judge and write off others when we don't want to deal with their unpleasantries, yet get mad when it's how we're treated first. We often fail to remember that just because someone has a history, it doesn't mean that that's who he or she is anymore. Especially because those who are willing to expand and grow because of what they've been through usually don't return to the past—often understanding that you can't run back to what hurt you in order to heal.

Letters To The Friends I Lost

In the midst of my relationship there were casualties. I lost two friends I don't know I'll ever get back. So, though I don't know if they will ever read this book let alone the letters I have written for them, I knew it was something I wanted to include. These letters as well as the people they are meant for will always mean a great deal to me.

S,

I don't really know where to start this. I'm self-conscious about what I want to say because it's been awhile, but I'm also not even sure you'll read this, let alone if you or anyone else would agree. I guess I just have to remind myself that I'm not writing it for any other purpose than to seal shut an area of my life you never really gave me an opportunity to close. Which is why I am sometimes a combination of both mad and upset that our friendship ended the way that it did. I understand that you believe "what I did" was wrong, but to be honest I don't really feel I did anything that warranted the type of response I received.

I understand that you felt it was strange that I was talking to someone you once dated. I understand it was even stranger how you found out. Not sure how to tell you, I was going to wait, and I felt that right then and there wasn't the most appropriate time. And to be honest, I had no idea if it was even going anywhere. As my friend you'd remember that my luck with dating in the past was always horrible and I felt I should at least get my bearings before I came forward, got excited, and told you about something that might not even become a real thing. But you noticing before I had a chance to tell you screwed everything up. It made it seem as though I was doing something I wasn't—as though in some way, shape, or form I was trying to deceive you by hiding it from you. And though I feel like I tried to assure you this wasn't the case, my feelings were still dismissed for yours. Your mind was made up. You felt hurt, wronged, and there was nothing I could do. But if I was doing something wrong I could have understood more of where you were coming from. Instead your anger left no room for me to be imperfect. It was I who made the wrong move. But I want to let you in on the real mistake because it's not what you think.

During the duration of my relationship there was a lot of alienation. Sadly, you were the first. But what got me while I was alone and upset that our friendship was over was that I wished I had someone to talk to about what I was going through. I wished so badly that I could tell you what you missed out on—a narcissist who took advantage of the kind of person I was and put me through hell and back. I wished so badly I could message you and tell you sorry—that our friendship could pick up where it left off. But it felt like you hated me. And what made me upset was that I chose all of this, thinking I had finally found something good, because that's what narcissists do—they love bomb you into believing they're everything you've ever dreamed of and then when they have you they take it all away, making you believe that at some point they'll give it to you again so that you'll stay.

So when I reached out to you toward the end of my relationship, thinking we might finally be able to have this moment of closure, I was hit with no reciprocation. You told me you had no desire to meet up and that you were just being honest. And though I appreciate that honesty, it still stung. It stung because I wanted to tell you how lucky you were. I wanted to express my sorrow. I needed to convey the story of what happened to me with someone I trusted and I thought that was you. But even without being able to tell you my story, it still felt as though you somehow dismissed my tale of emotional abuse. So though I know you believe I did something wrong please know that that something isn't quite what it seems. Maybe you won't understand that. Hell, at this point I really wouldn't blame you. Our lives are in much different places now. But regardless, you should know that there's a part of me that would still apologize. I feel bad about things ended. I really do. But then there's another part of me that says I did nothing wrong—that though you said this was weird, I didn't react that way when you dated blasts from my past. Maybe I should have been vocal about that because I thought that already defined our friendship because we never really fought. Which is why it hurt so bad when I was wrong. Because if I had betrayed you then every part of me would have had to make up for that. Every part of me would have been more than willing to apologize. I wish you could see or understand that, but you never gave me the chance. Even though I gave it to you in the past.

I hope that this finds you well. I hope that if you ever see this, it doesn't make you mad. I just had to free myself from words that were never spoken. And I can't be sorry for that.

X,

I want to paint a not-so-pretty picture for you. It's dark. I'm sitting in my boyfriend's car. We're talking when my phone lights up—bright enough to illuminate the space in which we sit. He asks who you are and I tell him. I tell him how we bonded over mutual heartbreak years ago and became really great friends in result—confiding in one another and being there when it felt like no one else was. But then he gets mad. He feels as though our relationship, though simply platonic over the last year or so, is inappropriate. His anger increases as he begins to think I've kept one big, giant secret—as if I had planned this behind his back and was never going to tell him about it. I'm baffled because this isn't something that I would do. But narcissists are good at turning things on you. I try to explain I hadn't said anything because our plans weren't solid and I felt no need to tell him, "Hey I may or may not be doing this thing soon, but don't have definite plans yet. Just thought I'd tell you anyway despite it being just a maybe."

So there's the picture. It's ugly, isn't it? In all honesty I feel like it is. But I know that I allowed it to be that way for too long. It's the main reason I disappeared. It's also the main reason I know we're no longer friends. I let the emotional manipulation I didn't even know was happening right in front of my eyes keep me from a friendship that always meant so much to me. Though I can understand how any sane person might not want someone to hangout with someone they've had a history with, I feel like there's a distinct line—a line in which both parties know if it's right or wrong. And I know you wouldn't have been a threat to my relationship. You would have been happy for me, but I never gave you the chance to be. My relationship somehow led me to some pretty terrible choices. And stemming from those choices lost me your friendship. I don't know if you'll ever read this, but I'm sorry. I hope you're happy. I hope you're thriving. And I hope that if one day we see each other on the streets we can smile and hug—erasing for just a moment these terrible things that haunt me. Because even if we go back to not talking at least we've had this moment. Our friendship, whether intact or dismantled, will always hold a special place in my heart because when it was broken you came along and helped me see it didn't need to be.

I extend all of my love to both of you.
Even if in the end it won't ever be returned again.

Once your friend,

Andrew

Dear Future Boyfriend

THERE ARE CERTAIN periods of time when a familiar feeling washes over me. It whispers that something needs to be conveyed—that my surroundings at the time are washing away simply because there's something I need to tell you. These letters are that something. And I hope one day you'll read them, because so much of me is poured into each and every word.

5.27.17
Dear future boyfriend,

Words have always meant a lot to me. It's almost like they make up various parts of me—flowing effortlessly through my veins and in every breath I breathe. Which is why I need you to communicate with me. Because despite all the time and effort I've spent working on myself, I am still scared that I will overthink everything. My mind will take me to figurative places that don't exist—places I never want to go again because, sadly, that's all I've ever known when it comes to relationships. I will think that you don't like this or won't like that. Unwillingly, I will watch almost every move I make at first. I will have moments in which I will flashback to chapters of my life that will make me feel as helpless as a child—making me flashback to less than ideal chapters of my life. And I know that none of this is an excuse for my behavior or to overthink, but just know that I will need your patience— that I will need your words and your communication that lets me know that you're not going anywhere. And to be honest, I don't think it's too much to ask to make me feel wanted. Because the more I feel wanted, the more I feel safe... and the more I feel safe, the more my love flows in return. I don't know if that makes sense, but I want us to share in that—the kind of love that always feels reciprocated. I don't want my moments of over thought to ruin what's in front of us and I know that with your love, your words, your affection, and your patience, I can build a bridge over the things I know I'm better off without. It's a project I will complete on my own, but that will benefit us both greatly. Because I don't need you to save me. In fact I don't need saving, but I want you to watch as the power of our love takes us somewhere we've both never been before.

6.05.17
Dear future boyfriend,

Sometimes I ask myself how it's possible to miss your presence in moments where it doesn't make any sense because you don't exist yet. And at times, I find the thought of you creeping into small areas of my life where you shouldn't be. It's not that I don't want to think about you, but it's that I believe in living in the present moment and the thought of you doesn't bring that or you any closer. And yet you creep into small, vulnerable moments where I in turn become impatient–where I wish you were here. These moments make me long for you, make me wish

I could reach out and touch you, because whatever it is that is playing out in front of me makes me want to share it with you. And just like that, as these thoughts begin to take over, it's as if the room in front of me begins to fade ever so slightly. The noise begins to muffle just enough and suddenly I'm somewhere else–lying in bed next to you, indecently. I'm painting you a picture of my surroundings—relying on what I think is memory to convey it properly. We do this often—bare our souls. It's different this time not because we think it is, but because it actually is. And though my body is mine alone I've given you permission to every part of me because you've done what no one else has. In a way we've each earned the right to lie by the other's side. But these moments aren't that of a sexual fantasy. We're sharing in an intimacy much deeper than that. We're listening, laughing, and enjoying each others company so much that it actually encapsulates what's really in front of me. I forget for a moment that this is a fantasy and suddenly I can feel myself being pulled away—torn from this now blurry vision of you. I'm back. And as I look around the room I realize there's still so much to tell you. I'm not sure what I missed while I was with you, but I know I'm lonely for these moments that don't yet exist.

7.04.17

Dear future boyfriend,

All my life, I've always felt like I've had to change for the people around me. Whispers that turned to screams taunted me—practically shoving the belief that I was un-lovable down my throat. So I wasted much of my own time trying to shed the skin I grew up uncomfortable in—not realizing that over time I was shedding the authentic skin of who I was and could be for a false belief. Because it's never been true that I'm unlovable. It's never been true that who I am will never be good enough. What's true is that others instilled this feeling in me—projecting their unhappiness and lack of good faith in themselves onto me. I felt as though I had to work to even be worthy of love and I hated myself every step of the way because I realize now that that's not how it works. I eventually realized that my perfectionist tendencies only hurt myself—setting myself up for disappointment time after time. I realized that as I watched my every move, my every action, and almost every word that I felt far more drained than I should. I felt like I became a mirage of myself instead of an image of the person I should have been. And I suppose I'm writing this particular letter because there are times when this old mindset creeps back in. It distracts me from what's in front of me by telling me lies. It makes me unkind not necessarily to you, but to myself. It whispers that the past survived and that I am nothing more than it. It takes me down a familiar road where I become blind to the optimism of actual truth. I will need your understanding because this fight isn't easy. It's like being at war with yourself—watching as one dark angel tries to kill your light.

7.20.17
Dear future boyfriend,

I always feel like there's so much I want to tell you—so much I want to share before you're actually here. I get caught up in words—sometimes repeating the same type of message over and over again because I want to make something clear. Things like, for so long my past plagued me. Others more so relay things like, please be patient and kind. But I guess hidden within the depths of my messages are another message—one indicating that the kind of emotional abuse I've endured has left me with a scar. And though I am a victim I am also a survivor. I've learned that I am allowed to be both simultaneously. It's why this book exists. I'm trying to use my words to not only heal wounds within myself, but also those that might exist within others because this kind of abuse is not specific to *just* me. Which is why if my stories, if my experiences, and words can help in the healing process of at least one person then I've done my job—I've done something right. But sometimes the vulnerability and honesty here gets to me. I can't help but think about the day you will read all of this. And suddenly it feels like my past is on display—my words, my actions, wrong doings of others, as well as my mistakes are being judged from behind a glass cage. Suddenly it's dark and I'm on display—fearful that when enough light illuminates the space in front of me you'll see everything I've been through and turn away towards some other, much prettier, display.

Still Worthy

One day I'll tell you my story
Of everything I've been through
But please don't look at me any differently
Cause I'm still me
Everything you dreamed
Everything we deemed
Still worthy
Just more than it initially seemed
And with it
A history released—washed clean
Lost time almost redeemed
Utmost honesty received
A new relationship finally meant to succeed
With nothing left to misread

Love Language

ⁱⁿⁱˡⁱⁿᵉ

READING *THE FIVE Love Languages* by Gary Chapman completely changed my life. It opened up a door to new territory I hadn't seen before because I hadn't been exposed to it, but now that I have I felt it was important to include.

The five Love Languages are:

- Gifts
- Quality Time
- Physical touch
- Acts of service
- Words of affirmation

Why is it important to know your love language?

We each have a specific love language that makes us feel loved. In a relationship, it's usually what makes us feel most fulfilled because both partners are getting what they need. However, we often attempt to love other people the way *we* want to be loved. In doing so, we fail to realize that though we're expressing love for our partner it might not be in *their* love language, which is how they're going to feel most loved and cared for. Over time, if we continue to love them in the incorrect way, they won't feel loved. It doesn't mean that the love isn't present, but that we aren't giving them what they need in order to feel it. And if either party isn't being loved in their love language, they're eventually going to feel that way.

How do I learn my partner's love language?

Like any language, a love language can be learned. Though it might feel foreign at first, we can actively learn to love our partner in a way that makes them feel most loved. And more so than just learning to love our partner in the way that they deserve, it also makes us feel good in return. (Chapman, 1992)

Thanks to Gary Chapman, you can actually find out your love language as well as more information about it here: http://www.5lovelanguages.com/profile/

Take Care

Don't forget to remember to:

- Take care of yourself.
- Take care of your heart.
- Take care of your needs.
- Take care of your emotions.
- Take care of your inner child.
- Take care of your mental health.
- Take care of your emotional wounds.

Don't forget to remember that:

- You should never settle for someone who doesn't take the time to understand how to take good care of you, but you also have to realize you have to take care of yourself too.
- Learning how to balance being taken care of in ways you've never been cared for, with the ways you had to learn to take care of yourself in the past, will feel foreign at first. Just because it's not what you're used to doesn't mean you don't deserve it.
- You're allowed to leave and walk away from mistreatment by saying, "Take care" and moving on.

Childhood

SOMETIMES OUR CHILDHOOD conditions us to believe certain ideas or thoughts about ourselves that are far from true—especially in adulthood. In some ways, they actually hinder our ability to form healthy relationships because we haven't taken the time to work through them. And chances are when we're in pain, especially romantically, there's a sad inner child trying to get ahold of us. It's our duty and our responsibility to let the child we once were know that we're here now, that the past can no longer hurt them, and that we will protect them in a way that they weren't protected in childhood. No matter how old we are, it's important to affirm our inner child. In fact, we'd benefit at any age from understanding and acknowledging this wisdom because when we do we understand why we're hurting. We're then allowed to give ourselves what we might not have been given in our childhoods, which is both encouraging and empowering for us in the present. But we must also actively work at being the person we needed when we were young—he or she doesn't just magically appear in front of us. We have to put in the work to heal the wounds of our childhood trauma, no matter what they might be, in order to be free.

A Letter To My Inner Child

11.21.17
1:35pm

I KNOW THAT inner-child work is hard for me to do, but I've got you. No one from your past can hurt you like they did. We're grown now, but when you're hurting, I promise I'll still hold your hand. And I understand that sometimes when you're hurting, it's because something in the present has reminded you of past traumas we've been through. But I'm always going to be here to remind you that we're okay now. It's all going to be okay soon.

Good Enough

WHEN DID I begin to equate my own self-worth with outside influences?

I never felt good enough for my family.
I never felt good enough around my peers.
I never felt good enough looking in the mirror.
I never felt good enough for the people I tried to love.
I never felt good enough when I wondered why they left.
I never felt good enough for current or potential employers.
I never felt good enough when the cycle would repeat itself again.

Growing up, I never felt good enough. There was always something someone else would do or say to make me wish I could change. Feeling this way, unfortunately, traveled with me throughout the years. From childhood to adulthood, shame directly influenced how I perceived myself. Not feeling good enough made me feel unworthy of love from sadly both myself and somebody else, which led to a plethora of problems in not just my life, but also my personal life.

But today I am affirming: I am, always was, and always will be, good enough.

Perfection

THE IDEA OF perfection has plagued me for years—seeping into the core of why I sometimes choose to be so hard on myself. But I have to realize that nothing will ever be perfect. I will never be perfect. No relationship will ever be perfect. And that's okay. Flaws are what give humanity room for improvement and in a bittersweet way I've fallen in love with this aspect of life. Self-improvement has taught me that there's more than enough room in my heart to give myself the things I was so unwilling to give myself in the past. And I realize now that the idea of perfection, of somehow attempting to erase the imperfect part of my humanity, was harming me. Unrealistic expectations of both others and myself put my life into an endless cycle of disappointment—making it hard to love myself when both parties involved couldn't rise to a practically impossible occasion.

Unofficial

I spent a lot of time in the past beating myself up and making myself feel guilty for not having been in an "official" relationship. I had only ever had short-winded flings that never lasted very long and yet I still felt the pain of the loss they caused me. These experiences sold me lies and I bought them—believing they were all I was good for. I felt like a transition between what people didn't want and what they wanted to find after me.

It felt like no one saw my potential—blind to what we could be together. And eventually, as this list got longer, it included myself. I began to dim my shine. I began to falter. What I wish I could tell that version of myself now is this: You are not a defect. There is nothing wrong with you—nor is there anything wrong in waiting for that one person who will finally see you for you. But you've got to get it out of your head that someone will save you. You've got to let go of the belief that you're not good enough yet—because no one's ever truly prepared for the kind of authentic love that unexpectedly finds you. But you also have to understand that no one defines your worth but you. You are allowed to be a force to be reckoned with… all on your own. You have more than enough permission to be both wondrous and a work in progress, regardless of the fact that someone didn't choose you. Someday that same person might regret leaving you and you'll laugh wondering why on earth you wanted to be with them in the first place.

I had to eventually learn that being alone is a strength and not a weakness. Because sometimes it means being unwilling to live in a world shaped by the norms of other people—by the guilt we sometimes experience when we watch others bask in the glory of their love while we've never felt more alone. So be patient. Use this time alone wisely. You can either focus on the fact that you're alone, wasting precious time, or you can go out and build something that's all your own. Use this time to get to know yourself because the only person guaranteed to be in your life forever is you. And when the day comes that real love presents itself to you, you'll be able to recognize it for what it is rather than what you convinced yourself it should be while mourning for the loss of those who so quickly passed you by.

Trust the timing of your life and, when it's supposed to happen, love will embrace you, leading you into the arms of the person who will continue to let you go places you need to go—this time together instead of alone.

Loneliness

LONELINESS HAS HARSH undertones. We live in the darkness of what feels like heartless circumstance. We feel fucked up, not realizing we only feel this way because we place so much of our self-worth into the hands of other people. It makes us feel less than fulfilled on our own and we often buy into believing that we can't be valid alone. But this thought process has got to go. It's time to realize that peace comes from within when you're willing to celebrate the strength of being alone rather than being with the wrong person out of loneliness. It's then that truth prevails, whispered lies wash away, and you no longer feel as lonely because you've taken the time to finally stand in the light of your own validation. This is when you win.

Loss

Sometimes the loss of a potential lover has the ability to feel all-consuming. It hits you like not just a brick, but a whole damn wall. For a moment you're breathless, powerless, and vulnerable. Every part of you aches for this person—no matter how large or small the duration of time you spent together. Every song paints a picture that makes you long for what was. It's hard to look ahead when you're only looking backward. And in that moment, you're only looking backward because you really thought that you had found it. But now you're drowning and the person you thought would be by your side has willingly gone missing. Yet it's almost like they're watching you thrash beneath the surface of the water and don't care. The current is made of misunderstanding and within its grasp you feel the ache of being misunderstood. Everything you thought you brought to the table was good, but they didn't see it. So now you're questioning if it's even there—if you are what you believe yourself to be. But loss likes to whisper lies. Your worth is not defined by this lack of love or the loss and grief that's come with it. Your grief, though valid, does not define you. And though the one that got away will always be that one *what if,* it's often better to leave it that way. Because though someday they might come back, it's almost always better to leave them in the past—rather than mourn the loss of an idiot twice.

Date Yourself

THERE IS SUCH a social stigma about going places alone, but I'm here to tell you that it's bullshit. Take yourself out. Get to know yourself. Stop feeling afraid that people are going to judge you. And stop feeling like you have to bury yourself in your phone if you're going to be out in public by yourself. Bring a book. Treat yourself to a cup of coffee alone. Go for a walk or a run. Go to a museum. A museum is *never* a bad idea. Chances are, no matter where you go, you'll learn a little something about yourself and the more you do it you'll begin to notice you aren't the only person there alone. Going out alone also gives you the opportunity to meet like-minded people. So it's time to stop worrying about what other people think by actively building the kind of self-love you've always dreamed of having. Because when we worry too much about what other people think, we don't give ourselves the freedom to be who we want to be. So date yourself. Take yourself out. Enjoy your own company, because when you consider the fact that you're with yourself 100 percent of the time, it doesn't make any sense to do any differently. Whatever it is you want to do alone—do it. Be authentic and brave in a world of people who claim to value these very things, but more often than not shame them because they're jealous of the free-spirited kind of soul you're learning to be.

The Fairytale

MOST OF US grew up watching the movies where Prince Charming swoops in and saves the day. The problem is that as we got older, we still waited for someone to come in and save us from our trauma. We expected our dreams to play out in front of us with little to no work on our end. We believed in the kind of love that could break even the worst of curses—watching and waiting, but somehow missing that this wasn't an accurate depiction of what authentic love is. What we fail to realize it that we have the ability to rewrite the fairytale, which then gives us the ability to break the curse ourselves—to pick ourselves up and ride off into a sunset of our own making. We don't need to wait for the love of our life for our lives to begin. And though it's true that love offers a greater sense of meaning and purpose in our lives, it doesn't mean that it's all there is. This means that the fairytale doesn't have to consume us. The idea of the fairytale no longer has to be our double-edged sword—simultaneously giving us hope while setting us up for failure. Instead, with the power of self-awareness, we have the ability to not let the poison sink in.

A Fantasy

FLASH FORWARD AND I'm in a fantasy. Instead of letting the person in front of me, whether physically or figuratively, show me who they are, I often imagine it instead. I envision our lives. And suddenly it's almost like we're standing there watching the sunset—our hands intertwined. But the crazy thing is that I don't just envision the good. I also begin to imagine every little detail that could go wrong—that has the potential to ruin us as a whole. I let my imagination run wild with the possibilities that feel as endless as the universe and the only thing that brings me back down is when reality sets back in. It's when they show me that who I imagined is different than who they are. And honestly, it's not always their fault. It's the fantasy... it's me. It's the fact that I didn't allow them to unfold in front of me and instead projected an image of who I wanted them to be. And I know it's these fantasies that keep my heart away from the true thing—from a love that's actually grounded in the utmost beauty of reality.

Know Your Worth

IF YOU DON'T know your worth, you unconsciously invite other people into your life who won't take the time to learn it either. Despite not even knowing you're doing it, this unconsciously gives people the permission to treat you in ways you claim to disagree with, but often still allow. However, when you're aware of your worth and know how you deserve to be treated, you never settle for less. When you know your worth, you stand firmly and powerfully in your belief that you are both worthy and valuable—never allowing the kind of people into your life who abuse and take advantage of those who don't.

Time

It's easy to forget how valuable our time is. Especially when it comes to romance. So if it feels like someone is wasting your time, they probably are. And the question you have to ask yourself in this situation is, "Do I deserve more than that?" When someone wastes your time, they're wasting moments you'll never get back. Wasted moments that could have been spent doing worthwhile things rather than dealing with someone who clearly doesn't value or respect you. Because someone who values you won't waste your time.

Distraction

THERE IS MORE to life than finding someone to date. Though having a partner in crime is nice, it isn't required. You have all the permission in the world to hustle on your own—to build a life that suits your wants and needs. So if dating becomes a distraction from this, from the kind of life you've always dreamed of living, then it's time to take a step back. Remember there's nothing wrong with dating, but your time is valuable and wasting it can throw you off course—distracting you from the bigger picture with something that's proven it isn't worth your time in the first place. Fewer distractions equal an undefeatable focus, which leads you exactly where you want to go.

Old Feelings

Five years ago I discovered gold
Learning that not everything is what it seems
That even though it gleams
It can still be fake
A maker's make
In my movie—two different takes
But now in 2017
I set the scene
A secret for just us to keep
A history almost washed clean
With the same drug I once had to wean
And no curiosity between
Cause instead of blurred lines
It's clearly defined
An hour after I walk through the door
With my clothes laying in a pile on the floor
Knowing full on what's in store

Minus this flashback
Because with eyes closed—everything black
Color seeps in—creating a crack
In a time continuum so quick that we're back
Wrapped in sheets of your old bed

A time that's now dead
And yet in my head
It felt like no time had passed
Except this time
You don't hold my heart in your hands
And now I understand
That from where I stand
I'm more than content
Giving old feelings consent
To no longer invent

The Gray Area

I'VE DUBBED THE gray area as that stage in "dating" where people really have no idea what's going on. It's that weird kind of in-between where you've hung out a few times, probably hooked up, but have literally no idea if you're dating. The advice that I always give to my friends, which I need to actually take myself, is that we're allowed to ask. When we're in this gray area of I-really-don't-know-what-this-is, we're allowed to ask the kind of questions that will help shed some light on the situation.

A lot of people don't ask these questions because they're not only afraid of the answer, but they're afraid that things will change. But if we don't ask, we're either allowing someone to string us along or wasting both parties' time. Sometimes we'd rather be left in the dark than actually label something, but personally I hate being in the gray area. I'd rather know what we are than putter around lost and confused—because nobody likes not knowing. So if this is you, all you have to do is ask. Or if you're content, which most people *aren't* when it comes to the gray area, then stop complaining about it. But if you complain about it, you probably care. So stop being scared and just ask. Because if someone leaves you over clarification of what the two of you are doing, then they've kind of just proven you shouldn't want to be with them in the first place.

Games

LOVE IS NOT a carnival. I'm not some game you can play, but darling I'm definitely the prize. And if you want to win, all you've got to do is treat me right. I won't accept head games that make me question my place in your life. Either you're in or you're out, 'cause I don't have time to waste and fuck around. And if that's the case, you can go play games somewhere else.

Change

Don't fall into the trap our own mind often sets when we're in pain from heartbreak. True healing begins when we change our mindsets from "I am broken" to "Everyday I am growing and healing." When we change our minds, we change our lives. And if heartache is good for anything, it's that it provides us with the change we often need. However, what causes us more pain is when we don't listen to it—when we try to hold onto our old selves. We dwell in that same pain—failing to realize we have to change *with it* instead of letting it change us into a version of ourselves we'll eventually no longer recognize.

A Choice

THOUGH IT MAKES sense that sometimes the circumstances in our life are less than ideal for a relationship, it does no good to consistently use them as a scapegoat. It snuffs out our power. Though we think there's power in saying, "I don't have time for this", it's actually the opposite. We're blaming outside factors—silently proclaiming that whatever's going on in our lives has more power than we do and that we don't have the God-given right to make a choice for ourselves. That's not to say that what's going on in your life isn't pressing or important, but that you can reclaim or keep your power when you say, "I'm choosing not to."

Why I Didn't Go To The Wedding

I'VE SPENT A lot of time debating whether or not to write this chapter. Was I ready to set a flame to everything that had been said? Was the bridge finally ready to burn? 'Cause with lighter fluid I stood next to you and explained everything that hurt me and instead you flipped the script—taking no responsibility for your actions and somehow turning it all back onto me. So I've decided I'm done tiptoeing, being taken advantage of, and placating people who have proven they don't exactly deserve my kindness.

I've realized over the years that love isn't always romantic. In fact, soul mates aren't mutually exclusive to that of relationships. And I thought I had that. I thought there was no way these people couldn't feel the love I had radiating inside for them, but I was wrong. My ultimate crime? I mistake I made in 2010. A year I did my own thing—branching off in college, making mistakes, and surrounding myself with the wrong people. I was unaware that this mistake many young people make would be cause for punishment, though it felt seven years late.

But for a while, in the past, I felt deserving of the punishment. I took the non-verbal lashings. Like never being there for my birthday—lying about working late and posting pictures and videos at a family party that same evening. The ignoring of a happy birthday texts in which I said I'd love to celebrate and then later seeing the celebration—just without me. The excuses and the lack of reciprocation that met my communication made my heart hurt. Though I understood that dynamics changed over the years, I still tried. That continuous trying eventually made me feel embarrassed because you can only grasp at thin air for so long until you look like an idiot. And I both felt and looked like an idiot.

It almost felt like I wasn't allowed to make mistakes. Especially when I discovered that this was why I was hardly ever met halfway. So I debated with myself for a while and made a hard decision. The wedding invitation sitting on my desk wasn't returned—a silent "no" that somehow screamed that friendship shouldn't be one sided. Why should I celebrate you when you've made it abundantly clear that you're unwilling to celebrate with me? I'm not naïve to the fact that some friendships die, but this was a loss I wasn't expecting. I'll treasure the years of memories, but it definitely feels like it's time to move on.

Burning Bridges

Through burning bridges
And cutting ties
I realized I'm not good at goodbyes
Only hurt myself holding onto the highs
Like they weren't all a guise
Cause through my eyes
It all turned to lies
A sort of painful prize
Because I grew wise
And made my decision
With no time for cries
Over what felt like spies
Foreign—no longer tries
And before the wedding bell chimes
I'll make my silent exit
Write this to vent
Cause with emotions spent
December 15th both came and went

Come As You Are

For too long I believed that if I had a better job, clearer skin, more money, was thinner or fitter, I might find someone who could actually love me. You see, everyone from my past seemed to point me in the direction, seemed to teach me, that I somehow wasn't good enough—that they didn't want me for who I was at the time. It appeared as though they didn't want someone with a little baggage or a past... and I had both. This way of thinking was extremely naïve, but I didn't know it at the time. I had convinced myself that my self-worth was determined by my rejection. I constantly tore myself apart in hopes that I might be able to put myself back together in a better, more appealing way. I wanted to be a diamond in the rough—shinier than anything else in the room. But wanting to do it for other people made it inauthentic. I wasn't doing it for the right reasons. I wasn't doing it for me. It was a defense mechanism in hopes that someone might not leave like all those who had before. I thought that if I strove for perfection, I might be more adored. Little did I know it was my heart's way of crying out for help. It was a cry that I ignored out of hope that my irrational plan might come true. But I'm more aware now of the healing that actually needed to happen. I'm aware of not only how far I've come, but just how much further I also need to go on this journey. And now, now I realize that if someone doesn't relay the message of, "Come as are you" then I want no part in the narrative it would create.

My Ex's Ex

DOING RESEARCH ON narcissism has probably been one of the greatest gifts I've given myself. Why? Because when my ex randomly reached out to tell me he was single, I knew it was a manipulative act. For a moment I sat around a table with friends in San Francisco quiet—pondering what this all meant. But then I realized that's what he wanted. He wanted to try to reel me back in. So I quickly replied with "sorry", but truth be told I didn't really mean it. All I could think about was my ex's ex. I couldn't help but wonder if he had been through exactly what I had been through. I couldn't help but wonder if he'd been emotionally abused and tormented too, but at the time I had to let it go. I regained my presence—going back into the brunch vacation mode I deserved. But to be honest, it wasn't long after this vacation was over that my mind drifted back to my ex's ex again. So not long after the nagging feeling made it apparent that it wasn't going to go away anytime soon, I gathered my courage and reached out. I was met with resistance, but after conveying that I had no ulterior motives, I made a new friend that summer.

Our friendship helped me reach a deeper stage of closure than I had before. And it helped validate my experience, because narcissist's thrive off making you believe you're crazy—by making you question your reality so much that it's trauma-inducing. And as we swapped emotional war flashbacks over tasty vegan food, I hope he realized that neither of us were at fault. We didn't deserve the emotional warfare or the abuse.

And now with a friendship forged from something broken, we can move forward into something new. We can relish in the fact that we're not alone, and that if our ex knew about our friendship he would throw the biggest, most ridiculous tantrum the world has ever seen. There's power in knowing that together, with our ex, we were much different people. Today we're better—more aware of the dangers people like our ex put other people through. Life is kind of beautiful that way, and for that I am grateful because I never would have guessed life would turn out this way—single, happy, independent, all while now knowing my true worth. And I hope my new friend feels that way too.

Me Too

I HAVE SAT here and rewritten this chapter many times. As a writer, it feels as though it has seen many changes in tide. But the one thing that always remained each time I attempted to find the strength to write was that I somehow still wanted to hide. I had never told this story to anyone, so it was difficult to find the right words to frame what had happened to me—what needed to be conveyed. This made it almost impossible to paint a picture to help come to terms with what I had experienced.

But then something crazy happened on October 15, 2017. #MeToo, a call to action for women who have been sexually harassed or assaulted in hopes that it would shed light on the magnitude of the issue, appeared on social media. For the most part, I feel like it did what it needed to do in order to inspire people to come forward—including myself, because it finally gave me the words I'd been looking for.

I was young. I was twenty-two. I still have questions because parts of that night don't make any sense to me. I was in the height of my party days, yes, but what twenty-two year old isn't? I could party all night, somehow evade a hangover, and go to work tired as all hell the next day and still somehow be okay. But something about this night seems different. Why would I later be shown pictures of myself passed out in a club where loud music was playing? Was I drugged? I mean, I wasn't with anyone that I normally hung out with. The young, naïve boy that I was, was attempting to make new friends with people who worked for the same company as me, but in a different building. So maybe I didn't know my surroundings well enough.

I know I'm telling my story with mainly questions thus far, but at least I've found the words to ask them, because those questions are what I'm left with. And I've always been afraid I'd have to say, "Be thankful that you're not the one who has to ask them."

The reason these questions strike me is because something about having to ask them seems off. Especially because at the end of the night, mere feet away from my own house, I came out of my blackout with someone I had perceived would be a new friend on top of me in the backseat. I don't remember saying yes. I don't remember giving consent. And if I had said it, then I was so far gone that I didn't remember it.

Some people would say that it's my fault—that I drank too much that night. But I don't remember drinking *that* much. From what I do remember I don't remember drinking enough that I would pass out inside a bar. To me, it just felt like something didn't add up. And the feeling of being horribly uncomfortable when I came out of my blackout seemed to indicate that something was wrong.

And yet, because of the social stigma that prevents men from speaking out about experiencing and surviving sexual assault, I somehow convinced myself it hadn't happened to me. I told myself that while I was blacked out, I must have said it was okay. But looking back at the incident now I realize that even that isn't okay. I told myself lies because I thought it would protect me, but all it really did was keep me from being able to mourn what I had experienced. And though this actually made it more difficult to find the words to convey my story, I'm glad I've finally found them in the midst of two much smaller, meaningful words.

Power

AFTER YOU LEAVE a toxic relationship, parts of them will seem like they've stayed. You'll notice that, even though their presence is no longer directly in front of you, it doesn't mean that they aren't somehow still inside your head. The toxicity of everything you had to endure, were forced to put up with, will sometimes remain. The habits they forced you to create to tiptoe around their madness will linger—eventually forcing you to develop the kind of strength needed to eradicate them. It feels like they've penetrated your mind in a way that has the ability to make you shudder—making you wish you could simply shed the part of you that ever let them in. But it's important to remember where the blame actually lies. This isn't your fault. Breathe—realize that the thought of them can no longer do any harm to you. And the good news is that the best revenge lies in taking your power back—in realizing that you are not what they've done to you. And it's okay if forgiveness doesn't come right away because, chances are, they aren't the first person you need to forgive anyway—you are. So fight on. Live on. And as you do, you'll eventually realize that they no longer have any power over you.

A Definition

ONE OF THE most powerful and beautiful aspects of love is that different people define it in different ways. But maybe if we're not getting the kind of love we feel we deserve, it's because we haven't given it a proper definition yet. Maybe it's not the intensity in which we're choosing to love, but rather the quality of both our thoughts on love and with whom we're choosing to share it. Maybe we let our mindset tell us that we don't know what we deserve—in which case we'll carry an infinite burden of weight upon our shoulders until we do. And when we allow those who mimic our lack of self-love and worth into our lives, we allow ourselves to be treated in ways we never imagined we'd experience. We let the world set the bar of our definition of love very low. For a plethora of reasons, we let our best intentions subconsciously make a mess of things because we didn't learn to love ourselves before we tried to love somebody else.

Emotional Abuse Vs. Physical Abuse

JUST BECAUSE IT doesn't leave a physical scar doesn't mean that emotional abuse is any less of a form of abuse. There isn't some unspoken feud between the two. They are both valid—each coming with their own spectrum of pain and trauma. Each provide a victim with a series of memories that they'd probably rather forget. And yet there are some people who believe that people cannot be emotionally abused—or that the latter is worse and somehow more valid. But let me repeat that *both* forms of abuse are valid and that this isn't some type of competition to see who has had it worse. Abuse is abuse—whether emotional or physical. And the victim who experiences either doesn't need someone arguing whether or not their experience was valid or really that bad. Just because someone might not fully understand emotional abuse or has never had it happen to them doesn't mean it doesn't exist. Nor does it mean that the people who have are any less deserving of support and recognition. Because it's this fear that society will somehow diminish his or her story that anyone who has experienced any type of abuse never finds the courage to speak up and share their experience—in turn causing a negative chain reaction of people never instilling hope in others with what they've survived and been through.

Damaged

RECENTLY WHEN I told someone about the concept of this book they replied with, "So cool! But whoa, someone seems to be a bit damaged by a nasty man in the past." I wasn't offended as much as I was floored. Who says that to someone, let alone someone they don't really know that well? Because I used to believe I was damaged—spending the better part of my younger twenties believing in the worthlessness other men left me with. It's only now, years later, that I realize just how much the mistreatment of others opened me up to a realm of real, authentic love for not only myself but for others as well. I won. I survived. I pulled through, maybe not unscathed, but with treatable wounds. Though there are still occasions when I have to remind myself of this, that I'm not damaged, I realize that inner-darkness takes time to fade. It doesn't just suddenly go away. It takes hard work to realize that there's nothing left for me here in this old mindset that still attempts to whisper lies I no longer have to believe in.

Note To self

IT'S TIME THAT you realize that you are in no way, shape, or form defined by the things other people have done to you. The mistakes you made in result of this pain may not have always had a valid enough excuse, but that's in the past now. It's time to put this part of your past behind you. You're allowed to forgive yourself for all the pain you inflicted upon yourself. It's time to remember that your worth does not stem from someone who is unable to see all that you've been, all that you are, and all that you have the potential to be. You are worthy of the world and if someone is unable to see that, then it's time to move on because grasping at thin air will never get you anywhere. Remember where you've been, where you are, and that you are strong, wonderful, and more than complete all on your own.

I Survived

I SURVIVED YOU. I made it through. And that is the best revenge I could ever hope for because there was never any intent to harm you. But if you felt harmed, if you were affected by my success and moving on, then that says so much more about you then it ever will about me. If you were enraged that I didn't need you, if you were angry that I could live my life better off without you, then I want you to ask yourself what that says about you. If you think about me and your blood begins to boil because I discovered my self-worth and left you when I realized I deserved better, then it was never me who was in the wrong—it was always you. I hope one day it hits you. I hope that one day you realize everything you could have had, but threw away with emotional abuse. I hope you *never* forget that I survived you, because I sure as hell won't. Because my survival was the win to a game you hardly ever lose. And to be honest I'm kind of glad I took that from you.

Stronger Now

THERE ARE TIMES when I feel haunted by these pages—like the very memories of painful times past have burned down a very important part of me.

Flashback and I'm standing in a field that used to yield a plentiful crop—flowers with a scent so strong they would somehow scream you're in love from the hilltops. But I'm standing in a field of ruins now—each monument a version of who I used to be before they got to me. It's painful to see, but somehow it feels necessary. Almost like I'm more than just stronger now. And yet, in my wildest dream I'd never imagine I'd be staring so vividly into the defining moments of years that drastically changed me. For years a handsome face with deceiving eyes would find me and we'd be happy for awhile watching the sunset a little too closely, until one day they'd be nothing but memories. And those memories would follow me around—making me miserable by default. They'd whisper things that could have been. They'd tell me how much happiness we could have had. But in hindsight, these were all lies. I'd been mistaken. However, it took awhile to realize my role in this haunting blockbuster. Though I'd been deceived, I also did some deceiving. I lied to myself—telling myself that this bottom of the barrel kind of love was all I deserved. So there I stood, more than willing to sacrifice everything for more than one monster in disguise—men who were only good for one thing. I'm sure you know what I mean. The kind of men who leave you lost in a sea of regret—tossing and turning so much underneath its current that it feels like even heaven can't help you now.

I realize now that a lot of my life was shaped by the strife that unrequited love caused me. It made me feel worthless, tired, and without a sense of purpose. I was bitter for years—feeling lost in that same barren field with ruins all around me. Because as more shrines went up, the further down I fell. I felt like I would never be good enough for anyone else, and in result I turned that same feeling in on myself. I became a cesspool of self-hatred because I felt like I could never be loved by anyone else. Shame consumed me and I lost what could have been the greatest part of me—a self-love so strong I could conquer anything. It baffled me as to why my bad experiences with love had seeped into areas of my life that had nothing to do with it. But they did. For some reason, they had to. It was obviously something I needed to learn. *All* of it was something I needed to learn—an unfortunate blessing in disguise that somehow led me to a better version of myself.

And one day when I looked down, I noticed a daisy growing from that same barren ground.

A Note From The Author

FOR YEARS I believed I was cursed. I felt used and abused. I often was, but even after everything I've been through I still believe in love. The difference is I now realize my role in what often felt like my own demise. I'm able to take responsibility for my past mistakes while simultaneously mourning the loss of "love" that was never really that great.

Being able to differentiate between covert abuse and love is a lesson in and of itself that might have been painful to learn, but that I will forever be grateful for. In a way, the future will thank this vulnerable and naïve version of who I used to be.

The purpose of *Unrequited* has always been finding freedom within the truth. I couldn't spend forever with what felt like my hands tethered to the past. It was time I had the courage to free myself from seven years of terrible experiences. And as I did, each word laid to rest what was once a very important part of my life. The pain of unrequited love no longer felt like a threat to my well being. I had survived the storm. I had pulled through without bitterness toward those who harmed me and instead let what happened to me fuel my art. It was freedom in its purest form. In a way, I've let most of it go. Something I wasn't sure I'd ever be able to do.

Because despite the harm most of the subjects of this book caused me I don't have any room for hatred in my heart. Hate takes up too much energy. Bitterness zaps any shred of happiness you try to hold onto you. So I had to choose not to give in to either. And I'd choose the same path over and over again if given the opportunity.

If you've read this far, I wanted to say thank you. It means more to me than you'll ever know. And if you liked this book, I'd love to hear your thoughts on it! Please leave a review wherever you purchased a copy. It does more good than you know.

And if you're interested in sharing any artistic snapshots while reading please use #UnrequitedBook as a way for me to find it and interact with you!

Again, thank you.

Book Recommendations

KNOWING AND HAVING a better understanding of love is important. On my journey of self-love and trying to discover what love actually is, books have greatly impacted my life, as well as my knowledge and definition of love. If you're on a similar journey, here are some books I found useful on my path of self-development and healing.

How To Love by Thich Nhat Hanh

Milk and Honey by Rupi Kaur

The 5 Love Languages by Gary Chapman (they even have a singles edition)

The Road Less Traveled by M. Scott Peck

Getting the Love You Want by Harville Hendrix

POWER: Surviving & Thriving After Narcissistic Abuse by Shahida Arabi

The Mastery of Love: A practical Guide to the Art of Relationship by Don Miguel Ruiz

Deeper dating: How to Stop the Games of Seduction and Discover the Power of Intimacy by Ken Page

Five-Minute Relationship Repair: Quickly Heal Upsets, Deepen Intimacy, and Use Differences to Strengthen Love by Susan Campbell and John Grey

*For Gay men:
The Velvet Rage: Overcoming the Pain of Growing Up Gay in a Straight Man's World by Alan Downs

Acknowledgments

THERE ARE HONESTLY so many people I want to thank.

The friends who have continued to believe in and support me, the new friends I've made who have wowed me with support, the old friends who have made it abundantly clear where their loyalties lie, the authors whose words on love taught me so much more than I knew before, the crazy experiences that helped shape this book, but more specifically the men who treated me so poorly I had enough content to create it in the first place.

To CreateSpace, for giving us indie authors a platform to release our work and put it out into the world. *To Greg Hahn,* thank you for the social media banners that advertised my first book. But also, thank you for designing the cover for Unrequited. You are so incredibly talented, my friend. *To my friend Mikey,* I not only get a kick out of saying I'm so glad I got you in the "divorce," but I also love collaborating and working together. Thank you for my release videos the first time around and I can't wait to see what we cook up with later projects. *To my friend Renae,* thank you thank you thank you for always letting me talk nonstop about writing. Thank you for editing this and being the first to ever read it from start to finish. I have valued your friendship for so many years now and I am so grateful to have you in my life. You were such a huge part of this book and I hope you know it would not be what it is without your help. *To God*, whose very definition is LOVE, I have sometimes struggled with the things I have gone through. But I know that they have happened for a reason—that reason being this.

To the people who helped me make this book happen: Terra Allen, Steven Beaudry, Garret Gloucester, Ashley Azevedo, Karissa Carriger, Jesse Baughman, Max Bilodeau, Casey Maphis, Felicia Quevedo, Briana Friedl, and Jessica Aragon…. words do not feel like enough. This book turned out as beautiful as it did because of your support. So from the bottom of my heart, thank you.

And if any of the men from my past are reading this I have to thank them once again. Without any of you this wouldn't exist. Through my misfortune and your mistakes came this book. But more than that, I eventually learned what I deserved. Your mistreatment only paved way to guidelines and boundaries that only enforce what I don't want—what each and every one of you put me through. More often than not many of you made me feel unworthy of love because you yourselves were broken, but damn did I make it through. Because though at one point I often thought I might never survive the pain, the heartache, and the loss I realize now that I was so much better off without each and every one of you.

And to you, my reader, thank you. It's hard to find the proper words to express my gratitude, but I will nonetheless try. Honestly, I feel like I could say thank you a million times and it still wouldn't feel good enough. For a writer, readers are the wind beneath our wings. We write our words to release ourselves

from a world inside our head that you in turn have the wonderful opportunity to learn from and escape within. And without
you our words would just be words. You help give them meaning
by not just reading them, but by interpreting them differently.
So thank you for contributing to our story. Thank you for reading. And in this case... thank you for contributing to mine.

References

Gary Chapman. *The 5 Love Languages: The Secret to Love That Lasts* (Chicago: Northfield Publishing, 1992).

Pete Walker. *Complex PTSD: From Surviving to Thriving* (CreateSpace, 2013), 3.

And after everything you've done
I can thank you for how strong I have become

'Cause you brought the flames and you put me through hell
I had to learn how to fight for myself
And we both know all the truth I could tell
I'll just say this is I wish you farewell

I hope you're somewhere praying, praying
I hope your soul is changing, changing
I hope you find your peace
Falling on your knees, praying

I'm proud of who I am
No more monsters—I can breathe again
And you said that I was done
Well, you were wrong and now the best is yet to come

'Cause I can make it on my own
And I don't need you
I found a strength I've never known
I'll bring the thunder, I'll bring the rain
When I'm finished—they won't even know your name

P
r
Kesha
y
i
n
g

Final Thoughts:
11. 27. 2017

Patience dear heart
I know you're still yearning
But there are days
In which I'm still hurting,
Reverting,
Flirting,
And Diverting
From the pages
Different stages
And ages
They spent haunting me
In a sea
Of my own making
With so much taking
But today
Today we're not breaking

Made in the USA
San Bernardino, CA
29 January 2018